IDLE HANDS, CLENCHED FISTS

Idle Hands Clenched Fists

The Depression in a Shipyard Town
by Stephen Kelly

SPOKESMAN

First published in 1987 by:
Spokesman
Bertrand Russell House
Gamble Street
Nottingham, England
Tel. 0602 708318

and 171 First Avenue, Atlantic Highlands,
New Jersey 07716, USA

British Library Cataloguing in Publication Data
Kelly, Stephen
Idle hands, clenched fists: the depression in a shipyard town.
1. Birkenhead (Cheshire) — Social Conditions
I. Title
924.7'51 HN398.B4

cloth ISBN 0-85124-436-X
paper ISBN 0-85124-446-7

Printed by the Russell Press Ltd., Nottingham (Tel. 0602 784505)

CONTENTS

Introduction: History Repeats Itself   8

1   Unemployment — The Crisis Looms   11

2   Life Among the Unemployed   16

3   The Politics of the Dole Queue   31

4   Trouble Brews   48

5   "We Want Work"   53

6   "Birkenhead's Communistic Reign of Terror"   65

7   An Unexpected Victory   77

8   The Trial   81

9   Questions in the House   87

10   Questions Elsewhere   91

11   Conclusion: How Did it Happen?   97

Afterword   101

References   102

For my father

FOREWORD

Work on this book has stretched over a number of years and has been encouraged by the guidance of many people. In particular I would like to thank the staff and tutors of Ruskin College Oxford who allowed me considerable time off from my studies to pursue this project. In particular Raphael Samuel and David Selbourne took a keen interest, giving me much valuable advice. I would also like to thank Professor John Saville of Hull University, and Edmund and Ruth Frow, who all read the manuscript and offered useful criticism.

Thanks are due also to all those, many now dead, who talked so vividly with me about their memories of the Depression in Birkenhead and especially my father who encouraged me so much.

Finally, thanks to all those who helped with typing and corrections including Joanna Sutcliffe, Valerie Taylor and most of all Judith Rowe Jones — also to Tony Simpson of Spokesman Books and the Birkenhead and Liverpool libraries for their help.

In the end, of course, I have to take full responsibility for any mistakes, misrepresentations or prejudices which might appear in the pages of this book. But at least a small cornerstone of history which might otherwise have been forgotten has now been recorded.

Stephen F Kelly
Manchester, June 1987

Introduction: History Repeats Itself

"History is generally only the register of the crimes, the follies and the mistakes of mankind."
Edward Gibbon

On the warm summer's evening of July 3rd 1981 violence erupted onto the streets of Liverpool. In the predominantly black working class area of Toxteth, which extends from the Victorian grandeur of Sefton Park with its university halls of residence to the decaying docklands and shores of the Mersey, unemployed blacks and whites launched a brutal assault on the Liverpool police.

It was an attack lacking any co-ordinated strategy though it was not without motivation. It was born out of the frustration and boredom of unemployment, with the police providing a target for the unemployed's hostility. Its spontaneity took everyone, including the politicians and the police, by surprise. With hindsight, however, they were later to admit that all the signs were clearly evident. For the one thing that the rampaging mob of blacks and whites had in common was that they were unemployed. And in Toxteth unemployment is as high as anywhere on Merseyside or anywhere else in Britain. Not that unemployment is something new to Merseyside. Unemployment in the area has always been twice the national average. But the sharp rise in the jobless which had arrived with the recession of the 1970s had seen unemployment shoot to a level almost as high as in the Depression of the 1930s, and in some cases even higher.

With one black in two in Toxteth on the dole, the stigma of unemployment was widespread. As ever, it was accompanied by poverty, bad housing and racism. The police, caught in the firing line, were blamed for the breakdown in relations with the long-standing black community. At the same time, they were made a scapegoat and seen as defenders of an economic system which had thrust blacks into deep deprivation. Racial tension between the black community and the police which had always simmered below the surface, was now out in the open as the two sides clashed in a vicious struggle.

For much of July, Toxteth was embroiled in a savage, unrelenting battle. Police reinforcements from Greater Manchester, Lancashire and Cheshire joined the Merseyside constabulary. The world's press looked on, with light-weight television cameras bringing the scenes of terror to millions as they followed the skirmishes along Toxteth's wide burning streets.

Politicians, community workers, sociologists, and pundits of all colours and creeds poured out thousands of words of condemnation, explanation and justification. It was, they claimed, the worst violence seen on mainland Britain in decades. Some even tried to comprehend how the people of Ulster after ten years or more of similar violence had managed to cope. Order was eventually restored to the once elegant streets of the city, but not before the police, fearing that just one more foray might finally overwhelm them, fired a number of rounds of CS gas.

The truce which has remained since has been an uneasy one as both sides have endeavoured to repair the rift. But as some commentators have pointed out, including Merseyside's Deputy Chief Constable at the time, Peter Wright, relations between the police and Liverpool people have never been easy. Indeed, there is a long-standing history of conflict and acrimony. For generations, Merseyside's police have been regarded with suspicion and, on occasion, with open hostility. Just once in each generation an explosion between the two has been enough to generate sufficient anger to last another thirty years or so.

There were those watching the rioting in Toxteth who had seen it all before. Indeed, you did not have to be very old to remember that in the autumn of 1932 those on the dole in Birkenhead had reacted similarly. For a week the town's unemployed battled with the local police as their frustration finally snapped. There were a great many similarities between the two demonstrations, and it is that which has, in part, prompted this study of the Birkenhead events.

As a young lad growing up in Birkenhead, I often heard references to the unemployed riots of the thirties. My father had many times pointed to the broken railings around the park, telling me how the unemployed had snapped the spike-tops off to throw at the police. The most bizarre reference I ever heard came during a student occupation of the Clarendon Building in Oxford in 1969. As the police appeared on the steps outside and prepared to disperse the students within, a lone voice yelled, "Remember the Birkenhead riots!" I never discovered who shouted those few words, but I wonder what he knew of the events on Merseyside almost forty years earlier. So much has been passed down to become myth while so little has actually been written about those events. The only references are to be found in some books on unemployment dating from the period. Most were written by prominent Communists, including Wal Hannington, and the brief mentions of Birkenhead are not always accurate. It is my intention to put these references straight, as well as to record in some detail the events of that autumn.

The events in Birkenhead, although receiving widespread coverage in the press and in Parliament at the time, were not necessarily of major historical significance. What is of importance is that they reflected for the first time during the Thirties the strength of reaction to continued unemployment. And although further rioting followed elsewhere in the wake of the Birkenhead disturbances, nowhere was it as violent or extensive.

The other aspect I hope this study will illustrate is that the violence we have witnessed in the 1980s is not new to Britain; nor indeed was it novel in the 1930s. Even in a small town like Birkenhead, political violence has often spilled onto the streets. Such violence is not limited to undemocratic societies; rather it has played a part in the history and moulding of most democratic societies. Whilst we may be critical of violence as a political weapon, we should recall that some of our most repressive and unjust laws have occasionally only been changed after violent pressure. Without the massive demonstrations on the streets of Birkenhead, the unemployed might well have been means tested for many more years. Similarly, how might we have widened the franchise without the demonstrations in 1832 for a Reform Bill, or furthered trade union rights without the protests against the imprisonment of the Tolpuddle Martyrs in 1834? Indeed, it is an irony that many of our most cherished civil liberties have been won not by the ballot box but by the fist.

What happened in Birkenhead was not new to the town, nor to Britain, and doubtless there will be similar disturbances of a political, social, or industrial nature in the future. What I have attempted to do is to provide some understanding of the problems of unemployment and the hardships faced by those who spent months and, in some cases, years on the dole.

CHAPTER ONE
Unemployment — The Crisis Looms

"If all the economists were laid end to end they would not reach a conclusion."
G.B. Shaw

As the First World War drew to a close, the dark shadows which had stretched across Europe for more than four years gradually gave way to fresh rays of hope. Thousands of soldiers, beginning the exhausting trek back home from the trenches of northern France and Belgium, hoped that a better life lay ahead. The politicians were rashly promising "a land fit for heroes", and after the horrors of trench warfare such promises were welcomed.

But it was not to be the case. The sudden return of so many able-bodied men to an employment market still geared to war rather than to peaceful trade caused an immediate glut. The result was unemployment. It was to be 1920 before Britain's economy was able to make the transition from armaments to consumer goods and thus boost employment prospects. Nevertheless, these few harsh years of high unemployment were sufficient to further embitter a generation of men already scarred by the experience of war. This bitterness was to manifest itself inevitably in a growing political consciousness. Many began to vote for and join the emerging Labour Party; others looked towards the example of Russia and joined the newly-formed Communist Party. In the 1930s, the political reaction was to be even more marked.

In the early 1920s, once Britain resumed her pre-war role in manufacturing and trade, employment prospects brightened, though rarely did the level of unemployment fall below ten per cent. The factories began to produce for peace-time once more; the shipyards were set to work constructing new ships for the Royal Navy and the merchant fleet to replace the hundreds of vessels lost during the war; and the rivers Thames, Clyde, and Mersey once again filled with ships of every nationality.

But the roaring Twenties, and the associated economic boom,

were not to last. In October 1929, a nervous New York Stock Exchange crashed overnight and the bubble of affluence suddenly burst. The signs had been staring Wall Street in the face for years, but were totally ignored. Fortunes were lost in just a few hours of trading and the repercussions were to spread like a shock wave through the industrialised world. Entire industries went into slump in America, western Europe, and Britain.

For much of the 1920s, business had capitalised on the apparent boom, over-producing when demand hardly warranted such frenzied production and speculating on flimsy foundations. The American economist, J.K.Galbraith later aptly described it as "the gold-rush fantasy"[1]. Finally the message had come home; consumer demand was static, speculation was over-optimistic, nobody could afford to purchase all the goods being produced. The panic of 1929 only exacerbated the underlying crisis, leading to an even greater fall in demand. Once the cycle was in motion, nobody knew how to stop it. The effect was to hurl thousands of unwanted workers onto the dole queues.

Between 1929 and 1931 unemployment in Britain doubled[2]. Even official government statistics, though highly unreliable and almost certainly underestimating the numbers out of work, showed that one person in five was jobless.

Table 1
Percentages of Unemployed in Great Britain[3]

1923	11.6%	1928	10.8%
1924	10.3%	1929	10.4%
1925	11.1%	1930	16.0%
1926	12.3%	1931	21.4%
1927	9.7%	1932	22.0%

The effects of the Depression were also seen in other ways. When Wall Street crashed, many private investors who had grown rich on the pickings of earlier years were ruined financially and several score committed suicide. In Britain the reaction among the wealthy was less dramatic; rather, it was the poor in society who shouldered the burden of the crisis through unemployment and deprivation. They had never been affluent, and any advance they may have achieved in the post-war period was swept away by the slump. Skilled workers, the unskilled and labourers all found themselves equally affected as machinery ground to a halt and factory gates closed.

The labour exchanges were ill-equipped to deal with the growing problem, and in many towns separate exchanges were set up to cater for different categories of workers. There were exchanges for craftsmen, tradesmen, and for white-collar workers, apparently seeking to save them the humiliation of associating with each other. Government funds ran so low that it became difficult to supply the necessary unemployment benefit and the Means Test was vigorously enforced.

Initially, the Government instructed all labour exchanges to demand that an unemployed person produce documentary proof of which firms he had applied to that week for a job. Without such proof there was no benefit. In effect it meant that an unemployed person could be continuously applying to the same firm for a job in order to have his papers signed. Inevitably, companies simply became tired of the same applicants turning up week after week when there was no hope of work and eventually they closed their shutters, refusing to see, let alone sign, the necessary papers.

This action forced many of the unemployed to roam from town to town on the lookout for a company that might still be willing to sign their papers. News of such a company was passed around the labour exchanges by word of mouth and it soon became common to see gangs of unemployed walking along the main roads in the early morning from one town to the next. They might have been hopeful that in another town they could secure some form of employment, but the effects of the Depression were so widespread that the chances were remote. Generally, the trek across country was simply to get papers signed, thereby securing some unemployment benefit for the week.

Frustrated by the hopeless prospects of finding work in their own towns, many packed their bags and moved to the more prosperous South. Families threw their belongings into a pram and, with the children perched on top, began the dreary journey to another town in search of work. Many were attracted to the capital, and London soon became full of destitute people, jobless, homeless and with nowhere to sleep. George Orwell, who for some time had experienced this way of life in London, drew on official records to illustrate the problem.

"The following figures published by the London County Council from a night census taken on February 13th 1931 will show the relative numbers of destitute men and women:
Spending the night in the streets: 60 men, 18 women. In shelters and homes not licensed as common-lodging houses: 1057 men, 137 women. In the crypt of St Martins-in-the-Fields church: 88 men, 12 women. In LCC casual wards and hostels: 674 men, 15 women."[4]

These figures add up to a total of 2061 men and women destitute in London on one cold February night. Thousands of others in London, meanwhile, were living well below the poverty line. The doss houses, or "spikes" as they were graphically known, had a huge turnover, keeping the unemployed continually on the move with their harsh rule that no one could spend more than one night in any one spike in a particular district. Nor could you stay in the same spike more than once every six weeks. Life in the spikes was grim, with callous wardens often robbing and cheating the trampers of what little money or possessions they had.

Although London had the image of a prosperous city, there was also widespread poverty. But at least the proliferation of service industries and small workshops made the task of securing alternative work less difficult.

It was the regions of Britain away from London which suffered the worst. On the Clyde, in the North East, South Wales, and on Merseyside the poverty which accompanied unemployment was horrendous. The wealth of these regions had been founded on single industries so that when they collapsed there was simply no alternative employment for miles around. In South Wales the demand for coal had slumped as industry cut back, while in the other regions it was the collapse of world trade that brought the ports to a standstill. Suddenly, there were no queues of ships in the rivers awaiting the change of tide, while the shipyards which normally rang to the sound of riveting had grown strangely quiet. Table 2 shows the effect on Britain's docklands as unemployment among dockers rose from 25.3% in 1927 to 39.2% in June 1931, more than twice the national average.

Table 2

Dock, harbour, river and canal service[5]

	Number insured . . . July		Number unemployed . . . June
1923	190,870	26.1%	49,775
1924	195,050	25.1	48,934
1925	190,480	31.5	59,948
1926	188,240	33.1	62,358
1927	180,760	25.3	45,767
1928	170,860	31.7	54,165
1929	171,220	31.8	54,377
1930	169,790	34.5	58,575
1931	173,090	39.2	67,837

In shipbuilding, the effect of the world slump was even more dramatic. Britain's shipyards, then generally regarded as the finest in the world, counted the cost as world orders crashed with the collapse of international trade. By September 1932 official government statistics showed that more than 62% of shipyard workers were on the dole, almost treble the national average of unemployment.

Table 3
Percentage Number of Insured Workpeople unemployed in Great Britain July 1st 1932[6]

	June '30	*June '31*	*March '32*	*June '32*	*Sept '32*
Shipbuilding & Shiprepairing	31.2	56.3	58.7	62.1	62.7
Docks	34.5	39.4	34.2	34.2	25.7
Total in all trades	15.2	21.1	20.8	22.1	22.7

In a Ministry of Labour report[7] published in 1932, the government was forced to admit that Britain's shipbuilding industry was in a critical state.

"Shipbuilding and shiprepairing continued during 1932 to suffer from more severe unemployment than any other industry . . . In the two principal districts — the North East and in Scotland — the percentage was over 70. New merchant vessels tonnage commenced during the year amounts to 72,000 tons gross compared with 200,000 tons gross during 1931 and 950,000 in 1930. The tonnage commenced during the first quarter was the lowest on record. The tonnage under construction in British and foreign yards at the end of 1932 was 225,000 tons and 540,000 tons respectively, compared with 401,000 and 1,003,000 tons respectively at the end of 1931. The figure of 225,000 tons includes about 143,000 tons on which work has been suspended."

On Merseyside, where the docks and shipbuilding formed the area's principal industries, the effects of the slump were tragic. Government figures put the number of unemployed in the region at 31% in September 1932[8]. In some areas, one man in two was on the dole. How they coped with the crisis is a story in itself[9]. In Birkenhead, which was probably the worst hit area on Merseyside, the unemployed existed on a day by day basis, making do with what little they had. It was a grim struggle which should not go unrecorded or be forgotten.

CHAPTER TWO

Life among the Unemployed

"Through squalid life they laboured, in sordid grief they died."
Robert Tressell

The town of Birkenhead lies towards the northern tip of the Wirral Peninsula, just a short boat-ride across the River Mersey from Liverpool[1]. At the census of 1931, its population stood at 147,946, an increase of only 150 since the previous census in 1921. Founded by the Benedictine monks in 1150, who built a sturdy priory[2] which still stands, it has always been considered an offshoot of Liverpool, and indeed that was primarily how the town came to be developed. As long ago as the 14th century, the monks were running a lucrative side-line ferrying passengers across the river, which in those days must have been a formidable trip.

In the 19th century, Liverpool began to thrive as an important shipping centre, founded on the slave trade, and the wealthy businessmen and merchants of the city looked elsewhere for their grand homes. The Wirral Peninsula and Birkenhead suited them perfectly. It was, after all, only a few miles away, with a regular steam ferry crossing the river, and its peaceful countryside was a haven from the noise and slums of commercial Liverpool. In 1810, Birkenhead was a mere hamlet with only 110 inhabitants. As more merchants were attracted there, so it began to develop its own industries, with the construction of a railway under the river in 1885 accelerating the town's growth. This supplemented the regular steam ferry which had been inaugurated in 1821. In 1824 an enterprising Scotsman, William Laird, who was a pioneer of iron ships, constructed a small ironworks and shipyard on the Wallasey Pool. But it was his son, John Laird, later to become the town's first Member of Parliament, who extended and developed the site into one of the world's finest shipbuilding and shiprepairing yards. As the shipyard attracted more attention and custom, so the town began to expand.

The docklands of Liverpool, which by the 1840s stretched the entire length of the river front, had become cluttered and unable to cope with the ever-increasing traffic in ships. Fresh resources were desperately needed for dockland, and Birkenhead offered the ideal prospect for expansion. In 1847, the town's first docks were constructed, and on 15th April, Easter Monday, Lord Morpeth formally opened the Egerton and Morpeth docks, before proceeding the short journey to Birkenhead Park, which he also declared "open to the public". It was an historic day for the new town. Although labour for the docks initially commuted daily from Liverpool, it was not long before they moved their families across the river to the new terraced houses. *The Edinburgh Journal* said of these developments: "We are impressed by the sudden rise of a new city in England. By far the greater number of our readers have never heard of this place, yet it is one of the greatest wonders of the age, and indeed one of those in which the character of our age is most strongly expressed." By the beginning of the 20th century, Birkenhead was a boom town[3]. Population experts were also forecasting that if it continued its present rate of growth, by 1970 it would be the largest city in Britain!

Like most towns and cities throughout the country, Birkenhead has its own history of violence. A number of violent demonstrations had broken out on the town's streets in the hundred years or so since the first merchants put down their roots around Hamilton Square. Many were the product of the social conditions of the time, with frustration bursting into angry confrontation. The constabulary often was unable to contain the anger, and was forced to call on reinforcements, either from neighbouring forces or, on occasion, from the military.

The first outbreak of mass violence was recorded in 1850[4], just three years after the opening of the town's splendid new docks and park, and at a time when the Birkenhead police force numbered just forty-nine men. The disturbances followed a meeting at the construction site for the docks. Quite why it happened was never recorded, but it may well have had something to do with organised labour. Police reinforcements from the town were summoned by the firing of rockets. The reinforcements duly arrived with cutlasses drawn, and the mob dispersed.

In 1857, organised labour was certainly at the centre of rioting when disturbances broke out at Thompson's Works in the Great Float. So serious were the riots that they could only be contained by the militia, which was called in to assist the Birkenhead police for the first time.

Two years later, following an election, "between one and two thousand proceeded toward Mr. Laird's yard in Church Street where an unprovoked attack was made on several of his workers as well as doing damage to a considerable amount of his premises". Five arrests were made, but within hours the crowd had reassembled outside the police station to demand the release of those detained inside. And the election? It was for the Burial Board!

In January 1860, rioting occurred following a fight in Field Street. Two men who had been arrested for assaulting a constable were later detained in the Bridewell in Hamilton Street, but shortly after their arrest dozens more turned up outside the police lock-up, determined to release them.

In 1862, the most serious rioting to that date broke out in what became known locally as the "Garibaldi Riots". That October, the Parliamentary Debating Society's monthly meeting at the Institute in Brook Street could hardly have anticipated that their seemingly innocuous debate "Italy and Garibaldi" would have provoked so much feeling. Yet hundreds turned up long before the hall doors were opened, and when the meeting did begin there was shouting, yelling and stone-throwing. Lamps were broken and a hastily-summoned inspector nervously decided to close the meeting. In the event, it was possibly the worst thing he could have done as it angered the crowd even more. And when a Roman Catholic priest tried to get the angry audience to disperse, it proved the signal for all their pent-up anti-papist feeling to let rip. The mob set off from the Institute to stone local Catholic churches. Churches of other denominations, in particular the Methodists, were also attacked — whether by the same crowd, or by retaliating Catholics, was never discovered. Eventually, the "Specials" had to be called in and, as in 1850, with cutlasses drawn and "1,000 good green-heart staves kept ready" they dispersed the rioting mob. But not before 55 police officers had been injured, 13 of them seriously, and 18 rioters arrested. Those detained subsequently appeared at Chester Assizes where they received heavy sentences, ranging from six months to fifteen years.

Another milestone was reached in 1867, when the force made its first call for help on the armed forces and navy. With an outbreak of violence from Fenians* predicted by the newly-

*Fenians were members of an association founded in New York in 1857 for the overthrow of the English government in Ireland.

formed Special Branch in London, which warned that both Liverpool and Birkenhead docks could be set ablaze, the precaution was taken of lying *HMS Donegal* in the River Mersey. In the event, the anticipated riots never occurred. Later that year, with the Fenian events still in mind, the police successfully appealed for all political meetings to be banned from Birkenhead Park.

In 1883 there were further religious riots when disturbances broke out following a Salvation Army parade in October. There were a number of serious injuries and further trouble was sparked off a few days later when one person was arrested and accused of stabbing two young women. By this time tension and antagonism towards the Salvation Army were running high, and when Captain Woolley, the movement's leader, later refused to obey a police order banning them from marching through the town, further serious rioting broke out. More than 2,000 demonstrators battled it out with the normally peaceful Salvation Army.

Twenty years later the traditional conflict between the Catholic and Protestant communities broke out once more when, in 1903, Liverpool police were called into the town following rioting at a crusade. And in 1905 an Orange band known as "Israel's Chosen Few" marched through the predominantly Catholic area of Park Street, which resulted in stone-throwing and fighting.

Racism also reared its ugly head that year, when 3,000 Birkenhead residents attacked four houses inhabited by Chinese families. The attack followed an allegation that one of the Chinese men had exposed himself to two women. But later evidence suggested that the rioting was inspired more by general anti-Chinese feeling.

In 1911, a local strike by railwaymen led to police from Birmingham and Nottingham being drafted into the town. But as with the dock strikes of 1879 and 1890, when violence was similarly anticipated, there proved to be no cause for alarm.

Serious riots occurred during the First World War when the majestic transatlantic liner *The Lusitania* was sunk by a German torpedo in 1915. Sailing from Liverpool to New York, *The Lusitania* had a crew that included many from the city and its surrounding areas. When news of the disaster reached Merseyside, anti-German feelings were unleashed on innocent and unsuspecting German families living there. Their shops and homes were stoned, while individuals were attacked and humiliated. When the cost was finally counted, there were 41 claims for damages totalling £3,180, and 436 special constables had been enrolled to quell the disturbances.

By far the most serious disturbances occurred in 1919 when the police went on strike in Britain for the first and, to date, last time. Although the strike was patchy throughout most of the country, on Merseyside it was particularly solid. Forces in Liverpool, Wallasey and Birkenhead came out to join the strike. In Birkenhead alone, 114 sergeants and constables stopped work, with the result that looting and mob rule threatened. On 3rd August the government ordered 500 troops into the town, where they remained for a fortnight until the strike had been broken. But, in the meantime, more than £15,000 worth of damage had been caused.

By the 1930s, the Birkenhead police force had grown considerably from its humble origins when just a few policemen could adequately guarantee the townspeople's safety. Now it was a force boasting more than 250 officers[5] and still expanding, for by this time the rich merchants, who had once contentedly settled around Hamilton Square, were on the move again, finding their plush homes just a little too close for comfort to the back-to-back terraced houses of the workers. Their sights were now set on such places as West Kirby, Upton, Hoylake, and Bebington as they initiated a further cycle of development in the areas outside Birkenhead's boundaries.

At Cammell Laird the state of the order book reflected the deepening economic crisis with orders for new ships well down on previous years, although the shiprepairing side was in a healthier condition. In 1930, eleven ships were launched with a gross tonnage of 61,257.[6] A year later only three ships went down the slipways, with a gross tonnage of 12,400.[7] In 1932, five ships were launched.[8] They were the *Royal Eagle* for the Steam Navigation Company; two small pilot vessels, the *Brook* and *Gurnard*; the Royal Navy cruiser *HMS Achilles*; and the *Hilbre Island*. Five ships were also completed that year: *Brook, Gurnard, Royal Eagle, St Andrew*, and *St David*, the latter two for the Great Western Railway Company. For much of the year Cammell Laird, with its 7,000 employees, remained hopeful that some of the £42 million pounds allotted by the government for further naval orders might come their way. And as the year drew to a close, their hopes were realised with an order for a submarine, a decision which may well have had much to do with subsequent events in Birkenhead that year.

At the beginning of 1932, there were 15,067 registered unemployed in Birkenhead: by the end of the year the figure had risen to 17,000. One person in three was without a job. In neighbouring Wallasey it was 4,463, while over in Liverpool 97,452 people were out of work. At its peak, unemployment on Merseyside was 31% of insured persons.[9]

In 1931, the *Daily Despatch*[10] had conducted a survey and reported that 1,120 families out of 7,000 were living below the poverty line, which they calculated as a weekly income of less than 7s 8d for a man and 6s 9d for a woman. The numbers below the poverty line worked out at 17 per cent in Liverpool, 15 per cent in Birkenhead, and 10 per cent in Wallasey. One out of every four families visited in the survey also shared a house.

In one particular way Birkenhead was different from Liverpool: its population was more Protestant than Catholic. Liverpool had been the centre of the influx of Irish immigrants during the 19th century. It was the nearest port of call, and unskilled labour was heavily in demand in the city at the time. Generally, any ill-feeling between the two religious groups remained beneath the surface, but it did show itself in certain ways. On the docks it was often necessary to find a Catholic or Protestant gang, depending on your religion. There were secret signs denoting your persuasion, which you could make to the gang leader choosing his team for that day. Employment on the docks was on a daily basis and entirely at the whim of the gang leader. If he didn't like you, or you were of the wrong religion, you would not be picked and would have to move on, hoping for better luck at another dock under a different gang leader. Work fluctuated, depending on how many ships were in the river. "Three on the hook, three on the book" became a common saying among dockers, meaning three days work, three days on the dole.

Housing also was open to corruption. Certain areas were Protestant dominated, others Catholic; and for a Catholic to buy or rent a house in a Protestant area was almost impossible.

For the unemployed, life was a monotonous routine. It meant going down to the Labour Exchange in Bridge Street twice a week to sign on the dole. Many went daily, however, in the forlorn hope that a new vacancy may have been notified. The queues stretched out of the Labour Exchange, down the length of Bridge Street, and as often as not, down to Hamilton Square Station, a distance of well over a quarter of a mile. It was said that the only secure job in Birkenhead was working at the Labour Exchange, on the other side of the counter. The only real hope for work would be if Cammell Laird needed a few extra men for a new shiprepairing job, but in 1932 that was a rare event. Even the Corporation cut the pay of its employees in August, with labourers and roadworkers taking the main brunt of the reductions.

Unemployment benefit was meagre, and in order to be eligible you first had to undergo the Means Test. At its peak, one million people in Britain were on the Means Test. Introduced to prevent exploitation of unemployment benefit, it was randomly used. Without specific guidelines, it allowed different councils to operate its use selectively and with varying degrees of harshness. Conservative councils tended to be tougher, demanding stringent conditions before benefit would be permitted. An inspector from the Public Assistance Committee would usually turn up on the doorstep of those applying for benefit, eager to scrutinise the contents of the home and the family finances before agreeing benefit. And if you were fortunate enough to have some private possessions, they would normally have to be sold off before eligibility for benefit would be sanctioned. It became a common sight to see pianos or furniture being humped next door for a friendly neighbour to look after when the Means Test Inspector's visit was imminent.

During the first six months of its operation in Liverpool, the Public Assistance Committee examined 29,793 applications under the regulations governing the operation of the Means Test. In more than 20,000 of these cases the rate of payment was reduced, while in 4,643 cases payment was refused altogether. In other words, five out of six applicants received a reduction.[11]

Benefit in Birkenhead amounted to 12s 3d a week for a single man and 10s 6d for a single woman.[12] But even this was not a standard sum set by the government. Instead, it varied from borough to borough as the payment was at the total discretion of the local authority. Rates for single men were much higher in some other parts of the country, as the following examples illustrate[13]:

Birmingham 13s 3d plus coal allowance. (66p approximately).
Bristol 14s.
Derby 13s — 15s.
Leeds 12s 6d under 21. 15s over 21.
Manchester 9s plus 6s rent allowance.
Northampton 10s — 15s.
Stockport 10s plus 4s rent allowance.
Walsall 10s plus rent and lodgings.

The allowance in Birkenhead of 12s 3d was a meagre sum by any standard and was barely enough to live on. A letter read out to the Public Assistance Committee in September 1932 from a 40

year old man gives some idea of his weekly expenditure, showing
just how far the allowance had to go[14]:

Room 5s 0d
4 bread loaves 1s 0d
½lb margarine 4d
¼lb butter 3½d
½lb dripping 4d
¼lb tea 3½d
Tin of condensed milk 2½d
1lb sugar 3d
2lb bacon 1s 0d
2lb meat 1s 0d
7lb potatoes 7d
Weekly amount for
second-hand boots
and clothes 6d
Tobacco 7d
Candles 2d

Total 11s 6½d

Balance 8½d

The diet listed in his letter was hardly substantial, making no
provision for fresh milk or vegetables, and the 8½d for "pleasure"
certainly would not go far.

Food was one of the major problems. A loaf of bread might
have to last three or four days and would often be stale by the last
slice, but nobody could ever afford to waste it. In the evening
children could be found hanging around outside the main
Cammell Laird gate on the New Chester Road, waiting for their
fathers in the hope that there might be a sandwich left in their
lunch packs.

There was little fresh meat, and what there was would be too
expensive. Six pennyworth of bits and pieces bought at the local
butchers would form the basis for a pan of Scouse (Irish stew),
and this would be expected to last more than a few days. If there
was no money for meat then Oxo would be used as a substitute,
with the dish becoming known, affectionately, as "Blind
Scouse". Pigeon pie was a particular favourite, needing only an
efficient method of catching pigeons. In one household sparrows
were caught in a trap on the yard shed and served up in a pie, but
it needed a fairly tough constitution to trap and eat sparrows.

Black puddings and bread puddings were other cheap favourites.

Allotments were popular with the unemployed. A small plot of land could be rented from the Council for a few shillings a year, and in this way the unemployed could add fresh vegetables to their diet. Many families kept hens either on their allotments or in their back yards, even though this meant keeping a careful lookout for poachers.

New clothes were a luxury, and few men owned more than one suit. At the Labour Exchange they would queue in old jackets and trousers, some in clogs, others in soleless boots that leaked. When winter arrived the only additional clothing would be a peaked cap and a muffler; nobody could afford an overcoat. Every Friday afternoon outside the pawn shop men and women would begin to congregate.

"The pawn shops always did the biggest business. There was a lot of them, and they were always jam-packed with things. Every Monday morning the shop would be full of people pawning their shirts or shoes and watches. It was the only way they could live. God knows what they would have done without the pawn shop. Then, on a Friday afternoon, when the dole had been paid out, you would see the men and women in the pawn shop getting everything out again, so that they could look decent for the weekend. The pawn shop probably epitomises the thirties more than anything."[15]

Wardrobe dealers were also a regular feature of street life, going from door to door, buying and selling second-hand clothes. Another regular visitor was the weekly cheque man, collecting his sixpences for the shops which ran a cheque system. This enabled the poor to purchase any urgently needed goods and then pay for them over the next few months. It not only ensured that children were clothed, but also helped make Christmas a little more luxurious. The rag and bone man with his horse-drawn cart and familiar cry was another weekly visitor down the back-to-back streets. He was in search of anything from old clothes to books or furniture, but didn't give much in return except perhaps a balloon for the children or a goldfish.

Women's time was generally occupied with looking after the family. Those who were not married usually continued to live at home, supplementing the family income if they had a job, or looking after the house if they too were unemployed. The extended family was a common feature, with married children often living in their parents' home along with any single brothers and sisters. Those married couples who did set up homes of their own rarely moved house more than a few streets away.

Families were large with most losing a child or two through illnesses such as diphtheria, pneumonia, or tuberculosis. With no National Health Service, a sick child would often go without medical attention until it was too late. In 1931, infantile mortality in Birkenhead was 86 deaths per 1,000 births, compared to 72.8 per 1,000 in 1925.[16] Tuberculosis deaths alone amounted to over 150. In 1932 an outbreak of rickets occurred on Merseyside, brought on by the lack of essential vitamins in the diet, and prompted a special investigation by the Liverpool Public Health Committee.

If a mother was fortunate enough to have all her children at school, then she would try to get a job charring at one of the large houses in the suburbs. Chars were cheap and plentiful and a popular status symbol among the wealthy. If a woman could not find work charring, then she would try to get some washing to take home, returning it laundered in the evening.

It was not uncommon for children to turn up at school barefoot or with the backside out of their trousers. If a policeman spotted an exceptionally ragged child he would take their name and address, not in order to prosecute, but to send a special ticket to the house so that the child could receive some clothes from the police benevolent fund. During 1932, 526 children were reported as being "badly clad" and recommended for financial help.[17] Some of the very poor were also eligible to get a dinner ticket for their children, which enabled them to go down to Price Street School for a free meal.

The tragedy of unemployment is not simply the poverty that it leads to, but also the loss of dignity and motivation that it entails. The structure that work provides disappears, leaving the unemployed with time on their hands and no foreseeable prospects. Some tried to commit suicide, and of the 24 suicide attempts in Birkenhead in 1932, 13 gave unemployment as the chief reason.[18] For a few weeks, maybe even months, being out of work might be a novel experience, but as time drew on and the chances of work receded, so it led to utter despair. Establishing any meaningful routine was difficult.

"It was the same day in, day out. In the morning I'd shout downstairs, 'What's for breakfast?' The reply would be 'toast', if there was any bread in the house. There was no paper to read, only an empty firegrate to stare at. In winter, we kept warm not by putting more coal on the fire, but by putting more clothes on if we had any. Then it would be down to the Labour Exchange. It would be unthinkable to catch a tram. We always walked, and each morning you could see hundreds of men all walking in the same direction."[19]

At the Labour Exchange in Bridge Street these men would join the end of the queue, often having to wait for hours before they reached the counter. Then with a shake of the head from the official behind the desk they would turn and leave. At least it helped to counter the accusation of "loafer" or "workshy".

Afterwards, they would stay and continue talking with their colleagues. Many didn't bother to trek home for lunch, but ambled down to the library to read the daily newspapers or simply to keep warm. As a consequence of their unemployment, many illiterate men used the time to educate themselves in the library, but this required considerable motivation and dedication. Others might spend the afternoons at their allotments or walking the streets. During the winter some might even wander down to the railway sidings with a bucket in the hope of picking up cinders or even some coal thrown off one of the trains.

Walking became a great pastime, partly because there was little else to do, but also because it provided some badly-needed exercise.

When men did find work, it was often the case that during the first few days or weeks they would find the physical strain too much after the long lay-off and inadequate diet, and this led to many premature deaths. When construction began on the Mersey Tunnel in the early Thirties, an unusually high number of labourers suffered heart attacks in the first year of building.

For the younger men there was the YMCA in Grange Road with its gymnasium. Under the supervision of the former international gymnast, Bob Lord, it built up a strong gymnastic team which gave frequent displays to the unemployed in the band enclosure in Birkenhead Park, or at Tranmere Rovers football ground. The swimming baths offered another form of physical activity but cost money, although the Livingstone Street baths with its cheap wash baths were regularly used by the unemployed, most of whose houses did not have proper washing facilities let alone bathrooms.

A recreation centre was set up at Beechcroft Hall in Whetstone Lane to offer leisure activities, but its possibilities were limited by its small size. Nevertheless, it did provide a useful service for the unemployed, who could spend their afternoons in the joinery shop making furniture for their homes. In the evenings the Council arranged for lectures to be given at Beechcroft on history, economics, and languages, but generally they did not appeal and soon ceased.

Every Wednesday afternoon the Claughton Picture House gave a cheap matinee performance especially for the unemployed. For many it was the highlight of the week. One regular visitor tells how he and a group of his friends had gone along to see a newly-released film. They paid their threepence admittance only to see a notice flashed on the screen announcing that the management had been unable to obtain the advertised film and were going to show another instead.

"Of course we were very angry at this because we didn't want to see this new film, we wanted to see the film that had been advertised. So we started kicking up a row. The fireman came over to us and started to threaten to throw us out and calling us all sorts of names. We told him to watch who he was talking to and just because we were unemployed didn't mean we were the scum of the earth. This was a typical attitude to unemployed people at the time. Anyhow, we told him to fetch the manager, and we told the manager that he shouldn't have advertised the other film if he knew he couldn't get it. Eventually, he offered to give us our money back, but we decided to stay and in actual fact probably enjoyed the film more than we would have done the other."[20]

For those out of work, the majority of evenings were spent at home, as drinking in the pub was too expensive. Nevertheless, drunkenness did increase sharply as some unemployed people found drink the only escape from the daily drudgery. There was little other entertainment in Birkenhead, except for the church guilds if you were religious, or the open-air political meetings which attracted large crowds.

Every other Saturday afternoon, Birkenhead's Third Division North football team, Tranmere Rovers, would be playing at Prenton Park. At the end of the 1931-32 season they had finished fourth in the league, just missing promotion to the Second Division[21], and during the summer there was much talk about the team's prospects for the coming season.

In one of their first home games of the new season, a large crowd of just over 8,000 turned up to see them lose the local derby against New Brighton.[22] But generally the crowds at Prenton Park remained small throughout the Thirties, with even fewer being able to make the expensive trips across the Mersey to see the football giants at Everton and Liverpool.

Any form of lavish entertainment was reserved for a Saturday evening when crowds flocked either to the Argyle Theatre in Argyle Street or the Hippodrome in Grange Road. One of the finest music-halls in the country, a couple of pence would buy a seat at the Argyle to see such stars as Harry Lauder, Hetty King, Will Langtry, Harry Champion and many other famous names of the day. It was renowned for its rowdiness and the reception it

gave the artistes. If the audience did not like them, they were told
in no uncertain manner; many a famous star was booed off the
stage or pelted with stale vegetables. It was always said that if you
could play the Argyle, you could play anywhere.

On a Sunday morning you could go to church, and if you were
not religious, there was always the Baptist Church in Laird Street
where the Reverend Alexander Stewart was not only a devout
Christian, but also a devout Communist, though not a member of
the Communist Party. Every day he proudly read his *Daily Worker*
and each Sunday he delivered his sermon with a sympathetic
message for the unemployed. As a result he was not always liked
by many of his congregation, but he attracted many newcomers
to his small, spartan church.

Sunday afternoons were devoted to the family, and this would
normally involve a cheap excursion to the seaside nearby or into
the country.

"We never had holidays. We would often go to New Brighton on
the train, which was about 2*d* or 3*d* return. Walking was the main
pleasure, especially on a Sunday or during the Bank Holiday. We
would go up to Bidston Hill and take a picnic with us. Sometimes
we would walk to Moreton. There was a footpath from Bidston to
Moreton in those days. We would spend the day there and then
walk back. This was how we spent our Sundays. It didn't cost
anything."[23]

During the summer those in work were treated to an annual
outing by their firm. The cost was small and the whole family was
invited and given a packed lunch. With few families able to afford
a summer holiday, this trip was one of the highlights of the year,
usually involving a train journey into North Wales from
Woodside Station.

"I remember once I had been out to Rhyl on the annual dockers'
picnic. We went on the train early one Saturday morning.
Somehow or other we missed the train back to Birkenhead and
there were no more trains. Anyhow, we couldn't afford to get a
train or a bus, come to that. So we decided to walk. There was just
two of us. After about four hours of walking we decided to kip
down until daylight. We found a suitable hedge and made
ourselves comfortable, when we suddenly heard this noise. It was
voices, and we then discovered that we were not alone in this
hedge but that there were about another half dozen people there.
They were all men on the move, looking for jobs. 'This is a good
place,' one of them said to me, 'but don't make a noise because
there's a copper's house just down the road and if he hears you
he'll shift us!' Obviously they had been there many times
before."[24]

May Day was another great annual event, especially welcomed by the unemployed. A demonstration was regularly organised by the Labour Party and the Co-operative movement, starting at the Haymarket and parading through the town on a circular route which brought them back to the Haymarket. There were always plenty of lorries and horse-drawn wagons, gaily decorated for the occasion. They drove through the streets behind the local trades union banners followed by thousands of children and adults. Various entertainments were organised including a walking-race from the Haymarket to Moreton and back, a distance of ten miles. Anyone could compete, and there was keen rivalry among the town's athletes to win this popular event. The Wirral Railway's football ground at the back of Birkenhead North Station was hired for a fair with football matches, boxing tournaments, and races. A famous star or celebrity was invited to open the function, and the crowd walked up from the town, following the procession before paying a few pence to join in the festivities.

Christmas was greeted with mixed feelings. Those on the dole wondered how they would be able to afford the celebrations, while the children eagerly looked forward to the carol singing, presents and food. But somehow everyone seemed to manage to have an enjoyable time, thanks mainly to the tontine (savings club), to which they had been contributing throughout the year. There were other ways of making a little money at Christmas time as well.

> "The menfolk, before Christmas, used to go up to Bidston Hill collecting holly, ferns, and bullrushes. They used to bring sackfuls home, and they would all get busy making wreaths with them. Their wives would take them over to Liverpool market on the Friday morning and stand outside for hours hoping for shopkeepers to come along and buy them. They didn't get much, and had to take 6d or, if they were lucky, 1s a wreath."[25]

Late on Christmas Eve it was possible to go down to the market and pick up cheap fowl and vegetables as the stallholders did not wish to hang on to them over the Christmas period. Over Christmas the food at home was appetising and plentiful, although presents were normally small and inexpensive. After Christmas Day celebrations with the family, Boxing Day meant a visit to Collins' Fair on Borough Road.

The official jobless figures for the Thirties only hint at the real level of unemployment at that time. Many men were too proud to go on the dole, particularly the white-collared workers who had never been on the dole in their lives and were ashamed and humiliated. Women also tended to retreat into the family home rather than seek work. The published figures do not include any of these people because they never registered as unemployed. The following is a reminder of what pride meant to one man: "My father was always a hard-working man. He had always worked on the railways, but had to retire early due to ill health. For most of the Thirties he was working, but there were times when he was out of work. He would never go on the dole; he was far too proud and thought that it was terribly degrading to go on the dole. Instead, when he was out of work he would get up very early in the morning, put on his boots and working clothes and go out and look for work. This generally meant that he would walk around the farms, travelling from one to the other and asking the farmers for work. In those days there were a great many farms in Cheshire, and sooner or later he would manage to get maybe a day or a couple of days work if he was very lucky. Instead of giving him money, the farmers would give him a bunch of flowers or a bag of potatoes, although sometimes they paid him cash. But getting a job always meant a great deal of searching and walking. In all his life he never once went on the dole."[26]

As 1932 began, the Labour Mayor of Birkenhead, Alderman Frank Tweedle, sent this message to the *Birkenhead News*, urging the unemployed to look on the bright side:

"1931 will pass out leaving unpleasant memories in the minds of many residents of Birkenhead owing to unemployment and bad trade. The dark cloud has not rolled away but there are signs of a break in some directions. That the break may be more sudden than we can see at the moment . . . is the wish of the Mayor to the people of Birkenhead."[27]

Although times had been hard for many throughout the Twenties, at least there was work and the prospect of a better future. But the Thirties shattered whatever optimism there might have been, turning many young men and women towards politics in search of a solution.

CHAPTER THREE

The Politics of The Dole Queue

"The meek do not inherit the earth unless they are prepared to fight for their meekness."
Harold Laski

The economic slump of the 1930s was accompanied by diverse political fortunes. The failure of the mainstream parliamentary parties to suggest any successful solution to the increasing crisis had already led to the formation of a National Government under the former Labour Prime Minister, Ramsay MacDonald. Designed to draw all parties into a pact, the Government of "national unity" only created antagonisms on the Left and became no more than a Conservative Party in disguise. Inevitably, it failed to resolve the crisis, the solution of which lay way beyond Britain's shores and way beyond Parliament's control.

But the failure of the principal political parties to offer any apparent solution left a vacuum which was eagerly filled by those with more extreme answers. For the unemployed these untried possibilities at least offered some hope, and it was hardly surprising that as the crisis worsened more people should opt for them.

Soviet Communism was one obvious choice. In 1932 it must have seemed an attractive alternative. After all, there was little mention of unemployment in the Soviet Union, and returning visitors talked enthusiastically of the great industrial strides being made there.

In Germany and Italy another political experiment was being born, and there were those in Britain keen to test its potential. But the emergence of fascism in Britain was only just beginning in 1932. Yet even in a small town like Birkenhead, the pattern of European politics could be detected. The same underlying political trends were at work.

For those out of work in Birkenhead, unemployment had come

as a shock. For years they had experienced full employment as the town boomed. The population had doubled to almost 150,000 in just under 50 years.[1] Although it could never be argued that Birkenhead was a wealthy town, during the 1920s it was faring considerably better than many towns in the North-West. But with the sudden slump in world trade, the town's prime industries of shipbuilding and the docks ground to a dramatic halt, and for the first time in a generation thousands of men and women found themselves without work. In contrast, Liverpool had always suffered high unemployment. Most of the work in Liverpool's diverse industries was unskilled and casual, with a rapid turnover in employees, so that shifting from job to job was part of the accepted pattern of most working Liverpudlians.

But in Birkenhead the need was for skilled workers for the docks and shipyard. When unemployment arrived it was these skilled workers who could find no alternative jobs. Besides the docks and Cammell Laird's, there were few other occupations into which they could move. The result was a large pool of skilled workers chasing too few skilled vacancies. The skilled unemployed in Liverpool had a far greater chance of finding themselves work as unskilled hands, due to the types of industries in the city. As a consequence, in Liverpool the pool of unemployed consisted mainly of unskilled men seeking unskilled jobs in industries with a traditionally substantial turnover in employment. These diverse factors shaped different attitudes towards unemployment.

In Liverpool unemployment was accepted as a part of everyday life, while in Birkenhead it was novel and the reaction was more militant. The militancy expressed itself in the development of a more organised Left whose fundamental aim was to attack unemployment. Three organisations led the campaign for more work: the Labour Party with its strong trade union and trades council affiliations; the Communist Party; and the National Unemployed Workers' Movement (NUWM), an offshoot of the Communist Party.[2]

The most effective of these three groups, both in Birkenhead and nationally, was the NUWM. It had been founded at a national level in the early 1920s, when British soldiers, returning from the First World War, had anticipated, and had been told to expect, a land of jobs and opportunities. Instead, they had found a country almost bankrupted by war, where their uncontrolled return to civilian life resulted in a massive surplus of labour.

In 1920, the Communist Party[3] was formed from a number of socialist organisations, and, as it confronted the problem of unemployment, it set up the NUWM to specifically co-ordinate all activities connected with the unemployed. Officially, the NUWM was independent of the Communist Party, and membership of it in no way constituted membership of the Party. Nevertheless, its leadership was dominated by the Communist Party, and there can be no doubt that its policy was directed by the Party itself. Yet it still received wide political support. The Trades Union Congress gave its full approval, while the Labour Party offered more tentative support. Provided the NUWM's policies and activities coincided with those of the Labour Party, it was happy to lend active support.

The principal force behind the NUWM was Wal Hannington, a member of the Communist Party of Great Britain from its inception, and a man who for much of his life was to be linked with the activities of the unemployed.

Hannington was born in Camden Town, north London, in 1895.[4] By trade he was a toolmaker, and for most of his life he was an active member of the Amalgamated Engineering Union (AEU). In his early political life he served on the London District Committee of the AEU; in 1920 he resigned to help form the National Unemployed Workers' Movement and remained its principal driving force until the outbreak of the Second World War. It was Hannington who stole the initiative from the Labour Party and organised so many of the hunger marches of the Thirties. He was initially a member of the British Socialist Party, but left when the Communist Party was formed in 1920. He remained an active member of the Communist Party till his death, and was one of a number of leading Communists imprisoned under the Mutiny Act in November 1925. He was a prolific writer producing numerous books on unemployment, many of them for the Left Book Club, as well as many pamphlets and articles. Between 1942 and 1961 he was a full-time officer of the AEU, serving as both an Assistant Divisional Organiser and a National Organiser. Within the labour movement it can probably be fairly argued that no one contributed more to the political organisation of the unemployed than Wal Hannington.

The NUWM grew rapidly, holding its first national congress in 1921 when between 70 and 80 committees were represented. That same year it published its own journal *Out of Work*, later to become *The Unemployed Special*. At its second national conference more than 140 groups were represented, and the position of the NUWM soon began to play a prominent part in Communist Party Congresses.

Not everyone was content to simply allow the Communist

Party a free rein in organising the unemployed, and in 1923 a rival non-Communist group was formed, known as the Unemployed Workers' Organisation[5]. Under its leader, G.A.Soderburg, it notched up some early successes, but in general the NUWM's organisation was too advanced, and within a few years the new organisation had foundered and disappeared. But it did have one important effect on the NUWM in forcing it to reconsider its promotion of the Communist Party. There had been early criticism of the NUWM's Communist connections by other groups on the Left, alleging that these connections clearly discouraged many from associating with it. The NUWM therefore began to play down its Communist links and stuck firmly to the question of unemployment.

Between 1921 and 1924 national unemployment fell from 17 per cent to 10 per cent[6], and coupled with the improvements in unemployment benefit introduced by the first Labour Government, this contributed to a fall in NUWM membership between 1923 and 1929. By 1930, however, membership was picking up once again and the organisation had been shaped by Hannington into a formidable opponent of unemployment, organising campaigns throughout the country.

In particular, it was campaigning against the Means Test, and for higher increases in unemployment benefit, which at the time varied from borough to borough. It was on this question that it was to have a great influence in Birkenhead.

While Hannington was a commanding influence in the NUWM nationally, one man was to have a similar influence on the movement in the town. His name was Joe Rawlings[7].

A slightly-built man, Rawlings was born in March 1894 the son of a miner in the Durham pit village of Wallington. While he was still a child, his father was killed in a mining accident, leaving his mother to bring up two young sons on a small pension. Two years later, an explosion in the same pit killed his grandfather and two uncles. When his mother remarried some years later, the family moved to Barrow-in-Furness, where Rawlings got his first taste of industrial action when his stepfather was involved in a long and bitter dispute at the Vickers shipyard. To avoid the recriminations and blacklistings which followed the strike, the family moved back to Durham for a short period. Eventually both Rawlings and his stepfather found work at the Cammell Laird shipyard and the family made its final move, this time to Birkenhead.

With the outbreak of war in 1914, Rawlings enlisted with the Ninth Battalion the Cheshire Regiment, and after twelve months' training was sent to France and the Western Front. Here his mining experience was put to use as he was given the unenviable task of laying charges beneath enemy lines. But the horror of war had a profound effect on him. By the time the so-called Great War came to an end he was reading any socialist literature he could get his hands on. Back in Birkenhead he soon found work again, rejoining his old company, Gordon-Alisons, and becoming a member of what was then the Friendly Society of Iron Founders. In 1920, this became the National Union of Foundry Workers, and it is now the Foundry section of the AEU. He also joined the Plebs League and the Birkenhead branch of the Independent Labour Party. When the Communist Party was formally established in 1920, Rawlings joined immediately. He helped to set up the Birkenhead branch and was to remain a dedicated member until his death 58 years later.

Shortly after being elected chairman of the Birkenhead branch of the Foundry Workers, Rawlings was sacked by Gordon-Alisons. It was a devastating blow, and for the next 18 years he was to remain unemployed. So, instead of organising workers he turned to organising the unemployed, and in 1922 he set up the Birkenhead branch of the newly-formed National Unemployed Workers' Movement. He soon became a familiar figure among the unemployed on Merseyside, speaking at meetings and helping to organise hunger marches throughout the area.

However, his left-wing activities not only made life busy, but also made finding work doubly difficult.

> "There wasn't work to be got and as a Communist you were debarred from factories on account of your desire to work among the workers to struggle. As a result you were out of work all the time."[8]

A mixture of people joined the Communist Party in Birkenhead. On the one hand there were those like Joe Rawlings, working class and unemployed, while on the other there was a number of middle class people who were fully employed and well paid. Many of the latter were teachers who had been converted to the philosophy of communism through intellectual argument, rather than through experience of hardship.

The Party's main recruiting ground was the Labour Exchange in Hamilton Street. Since many members were on the dole themselves, they were regular visitors and meeting those out of work was quite simple. They would hand out leaflets or sell copies of the Communist Party's daily newspaper, *The Daily Worker*, and there was no shortage of discussions and arguments.

Nobody had anywhere to go and time was plentiful.

Nevertheless, it was a hard slog recruiting members to the Communist Party. There were inevitable and, no doubt, justified fears that joining would make it even more difficult to find work. As a consequence, membership in Birkenhead rarely rose above 100 during the 1930s, and in 1932 stood at around 80.

> "It used to go up and down like that all the time. It was according to your methods and propaganda. How you would tie it up with their lives and make them see it was the Party of the future. Of course there was the Press shouting about the Moscow hold, shouting the usual pack of lies. All this had to be contended with. These were stirring days and you had the Independent Labour Party(ILP), the British Labour Party, the Communist Party, and a lot of National Socialist movements started up. All those meetings used to assemble on a Saturday and Sunday evening at Birkenhead Park gates and the Haymarket. Then there was a fight. The man with the most powerful oratory always got the crowd."[9]

Besides these open-air meetings, the Communist Party also held a private branch meeting each week, the venue for which was usually uncertain. It was reckoned the Secretary's hardest job to secure a meeting place. Usually it depended on an organisation or society that was sympathetic to the Party, but often it was a case of booking a room under a false name or in an individual's name. If the owner — as happened on numerous occasions — discovered that he had been conned into supposedly providing a room for the ornithological society, when in fact he was providing sanctuary for the Communist Party, he quickly turfed them out onto the streets. But there were some safe places where Communists could meet in peace and without worry or interruption. One such venue was the Bakers' Hall in Claughton Road.

Every Sunday evening the Communist Party, along with all the other political groupings, could be found holding their open-air meetings at the park entrance. Like Speakers' Corner in Hyde Park, each organisation had its own home-made stand or soap box, and one of its more prominent members perched on top to address the crowd. They were rowdy occasions and it was a favourite pastime in the town to attend. All shades of political opinion seemed to be present, with arguments often breaking out. At the Communist Party platform you could guarantee that a couple of plain-clothes detectives would be in the crowd keeping an eye on proceedings. At about 8.00pm, as the Sunday evening church services came to an end, a variety of religious denominations used to march into the Square accompanied by hymn-singing and brass bands. Setting up their pulpits alongside those of the political parties, they declared their own particular fervour to the crowds. Hymn-singing struck up, with the Salvation Army band usually drowning out all rivals. Up in the Haymarket, similar proceedings took place, with the NUWM turning out for one of its twice-weekly public meetings as well. By the 1930s, Joe Rawlings had established himself as the town's most prominent Communist. He was known as a fiery speaker and always attracted a good crowd around the Communist Party's platform to hear him dispense a few clever words of advice to Major Thompson and Harry Egan, his most noted opponents on the stands at the park entrance.

Occasionally, speakers of note came to the open-air meetings. Joe Rawlings recalled one such visit.

"For years on the Birkenhead Trades Council I kept a resolution going that Oswald Mosley should be banned from the town and that they should have no meetings in the Birkenhead Town Hall, and this was generally accepted by the working class in Birkenhead with the result that he never came into the town. The last time he came to Merseyside he was supposed to be coming to Birkenhead to address a meeting at the park gates. I didn't go down to that meeting. I was told to keep away. I was due to address a meeting of the Labour Party that night and of course I had put it to the Communist Party whether I should go to the park gates to speak, or carry out my commitment to speak to the Labour Party. And the Communist Party said, 'Well go to the Labour Party because if you go down to the park gates you'll get arrested.'

This Sunday evening everybody was tense waiting for Mosley to come, and the Birkenhead police organised the Birkenhead Park gates with a line of police right across — this side for Fascists, this side for Communists. This was the way it was prepared that night. Then the word came that while travelling through Liverpool somebody had hit Mosley with a half brick and put him in hospital. The crowd went off the deep end."[10]

Generally, the Fascists presented few problems in Birkenhead, mainly because the Communists and the Labour Party had built up a strong organisation which deterred them. The nearest the British Union of Fascists ever came was to Wallasey, a few miles away, where they held regular meetings at Moreton. Often a contingent of Communists from Birkenhead, led by Joe Rawlings, visited their meetings to heckle and join in the fight which invariably concluded the proceedings.

At their weekly closed meetings the Communists discussed problems facing the town. Unemployment was always high on the agenda, and details of NUWM activities were reported so that members were encouraged to go along to future events and participate. They argued for work schemes to help train those on the dole and give them useful work. Repairing roads and tram lines, or redecorating houses and repairing buildings were among the schemes most often called for, though these ideas always fell on deaf ears when passed to the Town Council in the form of a resolution. They also agitated for new housing for the homeless, and for new industries for the unemployed to find work in. Party members were also involved in local elections for the Town Council but, although they regularly put up candidates, their successes were few.

"The electors couldn't see eye to eye with the election of Communists as local town councillors because they somehow or other seemed to think his interests didn't lie in the town but in the Soviet Union, and you didn't seem to be able to attract them in the local politics or the national politics of Great Britain, or to vote for a Communist Party candidate. Yet they had all gone through the struggle and the line of the Communist Party was to organise the working classes and to give them a better life by overthrowing the system."[11]

The Party's propaganda efforts were always severely limited by a lack of funds. Leaflets were expensive to produce, and it wasn't always easy to find a printer willing to do the necessary work. Mostly, Party members concentrated their efforts on public meetings and activities at the park entrance and labour exchange.

One most important task was to sell the Party's newspapers, the *Sunday Worker* and *Workers' Weekly*, which appeared once a week until 1930 when they were superceded by *The Daily Worker*[12]. Every Sunday morning, Party members began the long circuit around the pubs in town, clutching bundles of newspapers. With the arrival of *The Daily Worker* their task became even more difficult. Only one in every eight copies was sold in a shop, so the remainder had to be sold by individual members. Early each morning, a couple of Party comrades were always outside the factory gates, particularly Cammell Laird's, before moving on to the labour exchanges. Lack of money made matters even more difficult, but the paper survived, changing its name many years later to the *Morning Star*.

Reading *The Daily Worker* was a dangerous occupation in itself, and anyone caught doing so was likely to be immediately branded a Communist. And reading it in the factory probably meant the sack for the reader if caught. Those who took the risk did so in hidden corners, or with the offending newspaper camouflaged inside one of the more popular ones. The Communist Party regularly invited guest speakers to address their meetings. One of the most popular was Leo McGree, the well-known Liverpool Communist and trade unionist. Joe Rawlings himself was also in demand by Party branches with invitations to speak in Liverpool, Blackburn, Wigan, and Manchester.

An outstanding public speaker, Leo McGree[13] was a member of the Communist Party from its inception in 1920. He was a joiner by trade, having served his apprenticeship in his native Liverpool before moving to Sheffield for a brief spell. But it was with his return to Liverpool that he was to make a name for himself, both as an active trade unionist with the Amalgamated Society of Woodworkers and as a leading member of the Liverpool branch of the Communist Party. Both these roles brought him into close contact with the unemployed and, along with Joe Rawlings, McGree had been instrumental in forming the Merseyside branch of the NUWM. For more than fifty years, wherever in the area there was a gathering of the Left, you would be sure to spot Leo McGree.

Surprisingly, there was a large number of women members in the Birkenhead branch of the Party, although not so many in the NUWM. Birkenhead was a town of heavy manufacturing rather than of light industries and consequently the majority of jobs for women were in the service industries, though even these were few and far between. The women who did have jobs tended to hang onto them, with firms usually more inclined to sack men rather than women because they paid women less.

Some Communist Party branches set up libraries where members could borrow left-wing books unobtainable in the public libraries. For a short period the Birkenhead branch had a library with pamphlets by Marx, Engels, Lenin, and Stalin, but as funds grew scarcer the library closed.

Raising funds was always difficult. Each branch was allotted a certain sum of money by the national party but more was always needed. A weekly collection of 3d per member went some way and was supplemented through public collections.

While membership of the Communist Party remained small, membership of the Birkenhead branch of the NUWM was thriving. Even though the subscription was 1d a week, it was reckoned the branch had well over a thousand members. At one point in 1932, so many were being enrolled that it became impossible to carry out simple administrative duties.

Not only did the NUWM act as a pressure group agitating for new policies; it also attempted to pursue forms of action which would radicalise the unemployed. Joe Rawlings recalled one such occasion when unemployed people decided to make their own rather amusing protest.[14]

"Birkenhead Town Council, apprehensive about the rising number of tubercular cases around the district, had decided to build a sanatorium out at Thingwall. The sanatorium was built and, on the day of the opening, the Town Council had agreed to go out there and celebrate the occasion by making speeches on the urgency and need of this sanatorium and having a feed. Well, I was going over to Birkenhead Haymarket this particular morning to sign on the dole and I saw a local politician haranguing the crowd of 200 to 300 outside the covered market. It was Major Thompson. He was standing on a limousine and had a frock-coat on and a Winston Churchill hat and a rose in his lapel. He had a huge placard on the side of his limousine — 'We Birkenhead ratepayers protest at the guzzling of the Birkenhead rates.' He said, 'I want somebody to move this resolution and we'll send it to the Town Council as a protest.' So I said (I was only young at the time), 'I'll move the resolution if you'll add an addendum, that is, that we do something practical about it because to just send a resolution to the Town Council it'll arrive too late, they'll have had the guzzle and nothing will have been gained from it. They'll only burn the resolution or put it in the wastepaper-basket. I would suggest that we line up,' — and we had marched umpteen miles in France and Belgium in the last few years conducting the war against Germany — 'surely we can walk four and a half miles to Thingwall,' and the crowd roared its assent. He said, 'My God, we'll all get arrested if we do that. You can't do it.'

Anyrate he got down off the limousine and we lined up and we marched out there to Thingwall. By the time we got there the Town Council and Aldermen had assembled in a huge dining hall and were going to prepare to have a feast. Of course, we gate-crashed. We got in the room, they flew out the back and got in the charabancs and came back to Birkenhead. We demolished all the food, lined all the men up outside, got ready to move to go back. As we were lining up a charabanc came full of detectives, so we gave them the raspberry. They couldn't do anything. It was a huge joke. We marched back to Birkenhead and there wasn't a word in the Press about it. The Chief Constable took no action."

That wasn't the end of the story either. A few weeks later a similar incident occurred.

"Well, a fortnight after I was going down Conway Street and a woman friend said, 'Are you going to the guzzle, Joe?' I said,

'You're too late, it was a fortnight ago.' 'Oh,' she said, 'I didn't mean the Thingwall guzzle. The Mayor, newly elected, has his first meeting next Wednesday. He won't have very much on the agenda. In fact he'll keep it very short. Nothing to discuss on it. Then he'll turn round and say, 'That's all the business for today ladies and gentlemen, we invite you all to the banquet.' And she said, 'Don't tell anybody, now get along.'

Well, I told everybody I could! There was about 150 to 180 lads turned up. The Council was open and you could just walk in; two bobbies on the door and the lads were going in six abreast because I told them it was a magnificent feed when the council was finished. The bobbies were saying, 'No good coming in here today, there's going to be no business.' The lads were all smiling and the air was electric.

We told the lads that as soon as he made his statement to rush out the back door to the big dining room. Well, then he came to the point — 'That's all my business for today, I invite you all to the banquet.' There was a stampede. They rushed along the corridors to the dining room and demolished all the food. There was a tidy crowd of us and it didn't last many minutes. They were taking handfuls. The Town Council was rather slow in coming along. They weren't in a hurry like we were and by the time they got there, there was hardly anything for them to get hold of.

The police didn't take any action over that either because that was another big joke. Everybody in the town was laughing and it wasn't even in the Press. But the Town Council at its next meeting moved a resolution that in future at all Council meetings, visitors who wished to attend had to have a credentials card signed by a councillor. There was a tremendous laugh over that. Thompson, the local orator, he was as usual out on a Saturday night at the Haymarket and he couldn't stand up to the laughter and criticism for his attitude. Ours was more practical. We'd got something from it and at the same time made a practical protest. They were the two guzzles in the town."

As unemployment increased, so the famous marches began. Organised mainly by the Communist Party under the banner of the NUWM, they proved to be one of the most effective forms of protest throughout the period. They were conducted peacefully, and brought home the message of unemployment to many thousands who lived in more sheltered and prosperous surroundings. Although the Jarrow to London Crusade is always recalled as the most famous of the marches, there were many others from different parts of the country. Joe Rawlings organised a march to London from Lancashire and Cheshire and some of the Birkenhead unemployed joined in the 200 mile trek to the capital.[15]

"There was a Lancashire hunger march and I marched ten men from Birkenhead. We had campaigned in the working class movement with leaflets and all the working class organisations and the Co-op supported us, as well as 12 trade union branches. Four Co-op guilds were able to rig the lads out with boots and all the necessary things for feeding the lads on the way down. The Co-op did a good job for us on the hunger march.

We marched over to Liverpool. It was pouring with rain and we were bedraggled by the time we got to Canning Street. There we met 20 unemployed from Liverpool and set off together. We started our march through Lancashire and collected various unemployed in the towns. By the time we got to Manchester we had 240 people with us. We had a little pipe band and a lorry and with these we started off the march. It took us nine or ten days marching and we collected £450 on the way.

We fed the unemployed like fighting cocks. Every town and city that we went through, the Public Assistance Committee gave us PAC provisions — margarine, beef, carrots, etc., and we used to supplement these things out of our own cash. We fed them like fighting cocks. When we were in London we marched round every afternoon. Hopley agreed to speak with the unemployed movement on the Sunday, a fortnight after we landed there. Hyde Park was absolutely full to the brim and it was pouring down. We couldn't hold the meeting. It was a terrible job. Anyway, Baldwin saw the writing on the wall and, instead of letting us march back, he agreed to give every man a ticket back to Liverpool, sandwiches and a cup of coffee. From then on things started to ease up and work came into the town."

As they marched, they sang to the tune of an Irish Republican Song':

Workers out of workshops and mines,
We are the unemployed.
From textile mills and factories,
The marching unemployed,
Tortured by the Means Test — we know our fight is hard,
Unemployed battalion of the Red Guard.

Hunger and mass murder is the lot
Of the unemployed.
Police attacks and batonings,
Our spirit won't destroy.
Glasgow, Bristol, Birkenhead
We know the fight is hard.
Unemployed! March forward!
Unemployed battalion of the Red Guard.

But it wasn't all grim and slog. The camaraderie that was built up led to many amusing moments. One evening during the early part of the march, they arrived in Wigan where the Public Assistance Committee had promised a hot meal. Not having had a decent meal for a couple of days, the marchers were driven on through the cold and wet weather by the thought of food. Unfortunately, there appeared to have been a misunderstanding and no meal was awaiting them. Needless to say, the marchers were extremely angry and kicked up such a row that the chairman of the PAC had to be dragged from his bed to offer his apologies. When the marchers threatened to throw him off the town's notorious pier he promised instead a hot breakfast of bacon and eggs for the following morning. The breakfast duly appeared and, well fed, the marchers set off again via the local market where the Birkenhead lads stopped off to buy 15 pairs of new boots, charging them to the PAC chairman.

When the marchers reached Crewe a few days later, a man appeared demanding to know who would pay for the boots. Apparently, an almighty row had broken out at the Wigan PAC when they were presented with the bill. Joe Rawlings told the Wigan messenger that he'd better be on his way back as they certainly had no money. To this day, they don't know who finally paid for the boots.

There were other marches as well, and groups of unemployed people from all over the country joined in, either from the start, or when the marchers passed through or close to their homes. On one such demonstration that travelled from the North to London, a dozen or so unemployed people from Birkenhead joined forces with colleagues from elsewhere. Although the following account was not written by one of the Birkenhead participants, it does give a vivid picture of life on a hunger march.[16]

"Today is the 13th and we have left Loughborough for Leicester, a distance of ten miles. Here we were received by the local Labour Party and taken for a hot meal in the Co-op cafe. Then we demonstrated in the town, marched up to the market and had a meeting, and then up to the grubber (workhouse) for sleep.

Breakfast was furnished at the grubber and at 9.30am we proceeded to Market Harborough. This place was entirely reactionary as far as local officialdom was concerned, and again we spent the night at the grubber after walking 15 miles. Food was pretty good, but one gets fed up with bully continually.

We left for Northampton next morning at 9.30 prompt, a distance of 21 miles and the toughest journey I have ever experienced, bitter cold and sleet all along the way. We stayed in a wayside pub for a dinner, which was a very fortunate affair considering the cold. At Northampton we were provided with food by the Labour Party, but, as the grubber had no sleeping accommodation, we had our food there and then slept at the YMCA. Next day we marched to Bedford, a distance of 23 miles, and we knew prior to starting that no provision had been made for us, but that did not daunt us, and so off we went, stopping at a small village to have our dinner in the Labour Party room. I forget the name of the village.

We arrived in Bedford after dark, and on entering the town the police inspector cried out "Halt", but on we went, taking no notice. I was itching for something to happen to break the monotony of tramp, tramping all the time. However, we fared fine considering the town is inhabited by retired officers and business people.

Started next day for Ampthill and we were again received by the grubber. I shall know the road procedure by the time this march is finished. From Ampthill we proceeded to Dunstable, a distance of twelve and a half miles. Here we met with the coldest reception of all, and after a cafe refused to serve us with tea for cash down, or even hot water, we managed to get all the boys in other cafes a dozen at a time for something to drink with their meal. However, having failed to get accommodation up till 6.00pm, we decided by the majority to proceed to Luton Workhouse, but a comrade here of no political or industrial connections came forward and lent us the use of her house which had five empty rooms. So we beat the reactionary officials after all.

Wal Hannington had met us on the way, and the petition to be presented to the Government was signed. Our next stopping place was St Albans; here we had a rousing reception after a short march of ten miles. On arrival, we were provided with a hot meal by the women's section of the Labour Party, and then had a real good time singing and dancing. Afterwards we held a meeting in the market hall where the secretary of the Labour Party said that they were solidly behind the marchers and their demands.

Returning to the Labour Hall, 32 of us were sent to a hostel where we had a grand bed and breakfast, and some went to the homes of comrades, while the remainder stayed in the Hall. Next day we marched to Barnet, a distance of eight miles.

On the approach to London the shortening mileage was noticeable. This was so as not to tire us on reaching the capital. Here we were received again by the Labour Party and we would have had a real reception had the whole of the membership been as class conscious as the president who, rather than propagate his extreme opinions, kept in the background as several reactionaries had threatened to resign. A meeting was held in one of the side streets, and then we had supper.

As no provision could be got for us in Finchley, we went to Islington. Here we were fixed up in the Co-operative Hall and were met by Communist Party comrades and Young

Communists, which was good after so many reactionaries. At night we demonstrated through the streets, held three meetings, carried posters of all descriptions, and made a great success of it. On the morning of the 23rd we marched about one and a half miles, held a demonstration, and then proceeded to Trafalgar Square, and oh, what a crowd! A pathway was made for us, the people saying, 'God bless you boys' and 'Good luck' and 'Well done lads', etc. The collection for the Yorkshire contingent alone was £45."

Another marcher, this time from the North East, also provided some memories which outlined the practical difficulties of marching for long periods.

"Many minor incidents stand out in one's cluster of memories. The night at Darlington for instance, when we resolved to send home a nineteen-year-old lad who had terribly sore feet. He was incapable of walking another step. But after learning of our decision, he was found sobbing bitterly in a corner.

Nor shall I forget the first bath I had in a workhouse. We stood in a queue outside the bathroom, and entered four at a time. The room was about five yards by three yards, and there were two zinc baths. Privacy, apparently, was unthought of. We undressed together, and two got into each bath. And all the time the inmate-attendant strolled in and out of the room, disregarding entirely our stark nakedness.

The soap was carbolic, of the poorest quality, and our skin burned and smarted. We dried ourselves on coarse, sack-like towels which rasped painfully over our bodies.

'But', as the inmate-attendant said, 'it's good enough for tramps, isn't it?'

The casual ward at Grantham also stands out vividly in my mind. A small room with bare walls and straw-covered stone floor, it was heated only by a small stove and the exhalations of our 90 men. It looked like nothing so much as an exceedingly comfortable pig sty.

Then all the other towns and villages in which the workers inspired us with fresh courage in our efforts: Leeds, where the Trades Council gave us an official welcome; Rossington, where the miners and their wives, hundreds strong, stood in the drizzling rain from eight in the morning until after midday to cheer us on our way; somnolent little East Retford, where the Labour women gave us two good meals and the use of their room; Shildon, where almost everyone in the little town must have turned out to line the streets and greet us.

And then the crowning welcome of 24th February. Who of us will ever forget the packed Square, the workers breaking through the ranks to wring our hands, the vast sea of faces round the plinth, indomitable old Mrs Despard giving us her moving *Caed mille failthe* (a hundred thousand welcomes), unfurling her green banner 'Ireland Greets the Hunger Marchers'?

That day amply compensated for all the rigours of the road. And we have the sure knowledge that our march has brought home to the people of Great Britain the tragic importance of the unemployment problem. Even our political enemies testify to this. It was at Peterborough that an old Liberal guardian came into our room and spoke to us. 'I know nothing about the march or its objects,' he said, 'but I do know something about unemployment, and if there is any way of rousing the nation on the question you have taken it.'

That we have roused the workers of the nation, the future will prove."

Again, there would be songs as they walked, usually to the air of a well-known tune but with fresh lyrics written by one of the marchers. The Scottish contingent would invariably march behind bagpipes and drums, while for other marchers a cheap mouth organ was the most popular instrument. To the tune of 'We are the Youthful Guard'[17], they sang:

From Scotland we are marching,
From shipyard, mill and mine,
Our scarlet banners raised on high,
We toilers are in line.
For victory we will fight;
We'll show our enemies all our might.

Chorus: We are the hunger marchers of the proletariat.
We are the hunger marchers of the proletariat.

We've met with Labour sabotage in village and in town,
But with the workers willing help,
We've smashed the barriers down.
This baby-starving government
Shall shake before our onward tramp.

We are the hunger marchers of the proletariat.
We are the hunger marchers of the proletariat.

And now the day of reckoning
No longer we'll endure
Starvation we have conquered now
And victory assured.
We are a strong determined band
Each with a weapon in his hand.

We are the hunger marchers of the proletariat.
We are the hunger marchers of the proletariat.

Marches, demonstrations and campaigns were all features of life in the NUWM and the Communist Party during the early Thirties.[18] It was all part of the attempt to radicalise the unemployed and promote policies which they thought would lead to full employment. It was against such a background that the Birkenhead branch of the NUWM began a campaign in August 1932 calling for the abolition of the Means Test and increases in unemployment benefit. This started as a local campaign, but ended some months later with national newspaper headlines, angry questions in the House of Commons, and stiff prison sentences.

CHAPTER FOUR
Trouble Brews

"The rule is, jam tomorrow and jam yesterday — but never jam today."
Lewis Carroll

For the unemployed in Birkenhead 1932 was a decisive year. It wasn't that the level of unemployment suddenly fell — that did not begin until 1936 when re-armament gave a boost to manufacturing industry — but that the unemployed began to take mass political action. For too many years they had suffered the indignities of the dole, the Means Test, and low levels of unemployment benefit. Idle hands inevitably became frustrated and looked for a political solution.

They knew that they had little or no chance of changing the economic climate. The depression was far too deeply embedded to be changed overnight; it was always going to be a lengthy process before the economy could be dragged towards an upturn. All that they could do was to tinker with the mechanism, which in effect meant trying to change the Means Test or to increase the levels of unemployment benefit. With this in mind they began a campaign aimed at abolishing the Means Test and at increasing dole money.[1]

The principal thrust of this campaign was politically inspired, emanating almost inevitably from the Communist Party and the National Unemployed Workers' Movement. At one of its weekly meetings in July 1932, held in the front room of a more prosperous member, it was suggested to the Birkenhead Communist Party that a demonstration and meeting should be organised under the auspices of the NUWM. It would be part of the NUWM's national campaign against unemployment. Most were in favour of the idea, though some doubted that the unemployed of Birkenhead would turn out in great numbers — after all, Birkenhead was hardly the centre of radical politics. But the plan was duly taken to the next NUWM meeting where it was agreed that such a demonstration should be organised.

Some argued that it should take place at a weekend when they could be more certain of greater numbers taking part. Others thought they should march when the Town Council was in session on a Wednesday afternoon, and present them with a list of demands. "They'd know that all the demonstrators were genuinely unemployed then," said one participant. The date was finally set for Wednesday 3rd of August, to coincide with the Town Council's next meeting. Joe Rawlings agreed that he would draw up a list of demands which he would present to the meeting for their approval.

Publicising the meeting presented its usual problems. In those days, neither the Labour Party nor the Communist Party had sufficient money to go in for lavish publicity. Leaflets were expensive, and local printers, like the local newspapers, were wary of anything with radical connections. To have your firm's imprint on a Communist Party leaflet wouldn't help to bring in work in the future. So, it was left mainly to the gang of chalkers who, when darkness had fallen on the evenings of Sunday and Monday, began their tour of strategic points around the town. Each chalker was allotted a particular area, and it was his responsibility to ensure that the message was well publicised. On walls, pavements, doors, and even in the road the message was clearly chalked up. "Unemployment demonstration 2pm Wednesday. Park Entrance." In the unemployment centres the word was passed on, while outside the unemployment offices there was always someone spreading the news. The Labour Party and Trades Council also announced the meeting and promised maximum support, although many in the town's Labour Party expressed disapproval of the idea.

On the day of the meeting, Joe Rawlings arrived early at Park Entrance in order to set up a platform from where he could address the crowd. As he approached from Park Road South, he spotted small gangs of men already assembling outside the Park's tall, ornate Victorian gates. Built in 1847 to coincide with the opening of Birkenhead's first docks[2], the Park was a splendid example of Victorian municipal elegance. It spread over a square mile, with lakes, pagodas, hills, and a cricket green.

Outside the gates, with their substantial edifices on either side which housed the park-keeper and his family, was a paved square. Measuring some fifty yards square, it was an ideal meeting point for processions and demonstrations. On a Saturday evening it was filled with soap box orators haranguing the crowds. Even a fair or two was known to spend its annual visit to the town at Park Entrance.

Joe Rawlings climbed up on to the granite monument and found a suitable spot from where he could best attract the crowd's attention, and then waited for the Entrance to fill up. By 2 o'clock almost 2,000 people had arrived. Most had walked in warm sunshine from points all over the town, but some had cycled in and stood about the square propped up on their bicycles. Small groups of children, now on their summer holiday from school, ran about the Entrance perimeter, excited by the assembling crowd. The police were also out in force, standing quietly in front of the gates, ready to listen to Rawlings, or drifting casually around the square. As he began his address, the crowd fell silent and only the sound of passing trams intruded. Even the shrieking children had quietened.

He told the crowd that it was not an occasion for rejoicing. They were living through grim times, and there wasn't much hope of improvement. We could fill this square a dozen times with the numbers unemployed in Birkenhead. Where would it all end? Mr Baldwin and his Conservative friends in the Government didn't seemed particularly bothered by it all, while some of Labour's supposed friends, like Ramsay MacDonald, had deserted them. It's about time we took matters into our own hands, he concluded, and let the authorities know that we are not going to sit by and watch our families starve to death. It's not just the Government who are to blame. Our own Council could be doing much more to help the unemployed.

A loud cheer greeted his words. After some debate and jovial heckling, Rawlings read out the following resolution which he proposed should be taken straightaway to the Town Council which was meeting that afternoon in the Town Hall.

"That this meeting of the Birkenhead workers, assembled at the Park Entrance, bitterly resents and condemns the present economics of the Birkenhead Town Council. We have witnessed the driving down to a life of misery and starvation thousands of workers, working class homes have been broken up, and evictions carried out.

We are determined, at whatever cost, to fight for the right to live in this land of plenty. Therefore we submit this petition signed by thousands of the working classes, demanding that this vicious economy drive by the Council should cease and that ways and means are found for employing workers in the town. We are not prepared to carry on living a life of degradation and poverty whilst on every hand we are confronted by the wealth we have created.

The resolution proceeds to make the following demands:
1. The abolition of the Means Test.

2. The abolition of the present policy of economy of the Birkenhead Town Council.
3. The extension of work schemes, including building houses, schools and road repairs.
4. We also demand that a Town Council meeting be called immediately.
5. A 25 per cent reduction in all rents of corporation houses and no evictions."

Not everyone agreed with the resolution. Some thought it went too far, but the majority seemed to think that they should immediately march to the Town Hall with it. A copy of the resolution which had been carefully written out was handed to one of the stewards and passed around the square for signing. By the time it was returned to the platform, 1,163 people had signed it. Some, naturally enough, were afraid to append their names to so radical a statement lest there might be some backlash. But well over half those present had signed.

A band of pipers, who practised regularly at one of the local unemployed centres, had been commandeered for the afternoon and were led out to head the march through town. More than 500 fell in behind them, and the procession moved off into the late afternoon sun across Conway Street and down Price Street towards the Town Hall. They marched under two banners inscribed "Fight the Means Test" and "Unemployed Workers — Struggle or Starve".

Although it was no more than a mile to the Town Hall, the march attracted considerable attention. After all, it wasn't every day that the pipes and banners appeared on the streets. Women and children stood chatting on the doorsteps of their terraced houses, occasionally waving when they spotted someone they knew or shouting encouragement. Near the Town Hall, however, their reception was not so friendly. Office windows were thrown open and some of those inside hurled abuse at the marchers.

Birkenhead's Town Hall, formally opened in 1887, was typical of the period and similar in style to many in the North West. At each side was a series of long steps leading to a balcony with a stone canopy supported by pillars. And inside there was all the traditional grandeur of carpets, chandeliers and polished mahogany.

The Town Hall's front looked out on to Hamilton Square, an impressive spot with neatly trimmed gardens, flowerbeds, and pathways. At one end there was a memorial to the dead of the First World War; at the other a statue of John Laird, the town's first Member of Parliament between 1861 and 1874, and son of the founder of the Cammell Laird Shipyard. Fine terraced houses hugged the other three sides of the Square, some owned by Birkenhead's wealthier citizens, others used as offices by the town's more prominent solicitors.

On reaching the Town Hall, five delegates from the demonstration took the petition inside to the Mayor, Alderman Frank Tweedle. They were invited into his plush parlour where they read out their statement. But the Mayor was not very forthcoming. Easing himself back in his leather chair, he agreed that the unemployed faced substantial difficulties and said that he had much sympathy for them. But he would not call an emergency Council meeting, although he did promise to place the matter before the next scheduled one.

There was little point in arguing further with the Mayor and, having listened patiently to his response, the delegation left. Outside they told the waiting crowd of the Mayor's decision. The crowd's reaction was predictably hostile, sufficiently so to give an early indication that something important was just beginning.

The *Birkenhead News* was not very impressed by what had happened that day, and in an editorial it made a scathing attack on the demands of the unemployed[3]:

> "While having every sympathy with the more than difficult times through which the unemployed of the town are passing, one cannot help but comment on the impossibility of the requests they have made this week to the Town Council. The conclusion to which one is forced, and it is a saddening one, is that the direness of their plight has caused them to lose their sense of proportion. The concessions for which they ask are tantamount to arrogant demands and it does not need a financial expert to realise that, if complied with, the town would be faced with bankruptcy in a very short space of time."

CHAPTER FIVE

"We Want Work"

"The poorest he that is in England hath a life to live as the greatest he."
Thomas Rainborough

September of 1932 began peacefully enough on Merseyside. One question on many people's minds was whether Everton were capable of winning the First Division Championship for the second year in succession, and how many goals Dixie Dean, Everton's Birkenhead-born centre forward, would score in the forthcoming season. The new season was just a couple of weeks old, and as yet Everton hadn't shown their form of the previous year. Birkenhead's own team, Tranmere Rovers, seemed to reflect the town's depression as they hovered in the lower half of the Third Division North, no doubt regretting that they had ever sold Dean to Everton.

Abroad, revolutionary strikes had broken out in Spain, while Gandhi was beginning a fast in India. In Birkenhead, the Cinema Film Committee had banned the American movie 'Scarface'; the Round Table had just held its annual dinner; on the first Saturday in the month, the YMCA gymnasts had given a well-attended display in the band enclosure; and the last of the popular summer sailings from Liverpool to Llandudno was scheduled, fare six shillings for a day return. Will Langtry was appearing at the famous Argyle Theatre, while over at the Empire in Liverpool you could see Ivor Novello in 'I Lived With You'.

In Lancashire, textile workers were on strike, and the Birkenhead Trades Council had inserted an advert in the *Birkenhead News* in support of their struggle[1].

"The textile workers of Lancashire are engaged in a struggle for the right to live. They are threatened with starvation. To those who feel these men and women are fighting justly for their families and homes, this appeal is made for donations to the food fund. Contributions, however small, will be received gratefully by Alderman W Egan, 36 Hamilton Street. Who gives quickly gives twice."

Generally, the events of 3rd August at the Park Entrance and the Town Hall were quickly forgotten, though a timely reminder, in the form of a letter, appeared in the *Birkenhead News* a few weeks after the demonstration.[2]

"Sir,
In your report of the demonstration to present the petition to the Mayor against the Means Test, I was particularly struck by the remarkable assertions by the Chairman of the PAC, Mr A W Baker, in his statement to the *Advertiser*. Mr Baker says, 'The Means Test or strictly speaking the Needs Test is working very well. A man with no means of living has nothing to fear at all.' The last part of this statement is simply a cold blooded untruth. And to call the atrocious measures a 'Needs Test' is a callous cynicism. Even if a person gets the rate of 15s. 3d., that is not representative of his needs. It means 2s. 2d. per day for food, clothing, accommodation, medicine and Christianity! (Not to mention cultural and recreational amenities.) In practice the majority of applicants are getting less than the maximum rate, their relatives having to maintain them wholly or partly out of their own inadequate wages. The Means Test is obviously not designed to cater for needs, or the benefit paid would have been increased in 99 per cent of cases. It is designed, as G K Chesterton put it, 'To kick those who are clinging by their fingernails to the edge of the chasm, into the chasm.' We are living in a land reeking with wealth and overflowing with plenty. The class which Mr Baker serves so well in their opulence and greed, are in truth, sowing the wind and will assuredly reap the whirlwind.
Yours etc.
Blood-Red Bolshevik"

Behind the scenes, plans had been made for a massive march on the Town Hall. It was scheduled for Wednesday 7th September, to coincide with the next meeting of the Town Council when the unemployed's demands were to be heard. The chalkers were sent out again, taking care to dodge the police who were becoming evermore suspicious of Joe Rawlings and his comrades. As before, the march was to begin at 2pm at the Park Entrance.

This time there was little need for the NUWM's leaders to spend time haranguing the crowd. Best to get on with the march, they thought, and maybe have speeches at the Town Hall when we know what's going on. The same band of pipers turned up to lead the march, resplendent in their colourful kilts, carefully kept despite the hard times. And shortly after two o'clock they moved off, followed by some 3,000 unemployed. Their mood seemed cheerful though determined. It was at least something to look forward to, and it broke the otherwise monotonous routine.

When they arrived at the Town Hall, a delegation of NUWM leaders once more left the crowd and went inside to talk with the Mayor. This time, however, the Mayor was not in a welcoming mood. He'd clearly had enough of them after the last visit and refused even to see them. The delegation angrily stormed out of the building, accompanied by the police. One of them climbed on a wall and began to tell the crowd what had happened. "They're not interested in us," he shouted, "they can't even be bothered to talk to us." The crowd, which was growing all the time, became angry. Someone shouted "What are we supposed to do, starve?", and a chant struck up of "Down with the Means Test!" By now more than 5,000 people had gathered in Hamilton Square and they were spreading out across the roads and onto the grass. Windows around the Square had been opened and people inside looked out, curious to know what was going on.

Leo McGree, the Communist Party activist from across the Mersey in Liverpool, told the crowd from the Town Hall steps, "We will remain here till we get an answer." There was a roar of approval at this, and McGree led them in a chorus of the Red Flag. It was like election night.

Just as their singing ended, a well-known Labour Councillor in the town, Alderman Charlie McVey, arrived at the Town Hall with a delegation from the National Union of Dockers. There were some cheers when it was learnt that they had come in support, to protest against the Means Test. But the cheers suddenly turned to amazement when McVey and his men walked past the NUWM leaders and marched up the Town Hall steps and through the doors, where they were admitted by the police.

"We want to see the Mayor as well," cried the crowd. But it turned out that the dockers had made an appointment to see the Mayor, so that he was obliged to meet with them. As they left, however, the dockers urged the Mayor to talk with the unemployed, and he reluctantly agreed. A policeman was sent outside to invite a delegation from the demonstration inside. McGree was overjoyed. "We've got what we wanted by refusing to go" he shouted to the crowd. But inside the Mayor's parlour once more it was the same story as before — a promise to place their demands before the Town Council. "I can do little else," pleaded the Mayor.

Reporting back to the crowd outside, Joe Rawlings promised a further march on the Town Hall. "Next time we'll make them listen," he yelled, "and we won't be fobbed off like we have been today."

As McGree and Rawlings wandered away into the late afternoon, and the large crowd dispersed towards Woodside to catch their trams home, they wondered how they could ever get the Council even to consider their demands. "Is there anything else we could do? Perhaps we ought to talk with the Labour Councillors," they thought, knowing full well that they wouldn't have much sympathy for Communist Party members.

As arranged, the unemployed next assembled at the Park Entrance on the windy afternoon of Tuesday 13th September.[3] The day showed all the signs of the approaching autumn as the leaves and dirt swirled around the open streets about the entrance. Opposite, a queue was gathering outside the Gaumont cinema, waiting for the matinee performance.

In the preceding days, Rawlings and McGree had been busy. They had seen a number of prominent Socialists and Labour followers in the town, and had secured their support by enlisting a number of them to address the unemployed. They were determined that today's march would be something of an event.

A crowd of 3,000 had already congregated by two o'clock, some better wrapped against the biting wind than others. Lining up four abreast, though this time without the pipe band, they marched off under a colourful banner emblazoned "Unemployed Workers — Struggle or Starve". Another contingent set off from Rock Ferry and New Ferry, also bound for the Town Hall.

The approach to the Town Hall had by this time become such a well-trodden route that any variation was to be welcomed. Both demonstrations had begun peacefully, in the company of not very many policemen.

But the general good humour of the previous weeks was to be short-lived. The approach to the Means Test offices in Hamilton Street brought the first hint of militancy. Those heading the long procession turned towards the office and, catching sight of some of the more unpopular officials, began to yell and shout abuse at them. Their example was followed by others, and for some minutes there was a hubbub which could be heard outside the Town Hall, nearly half a mile away.

When the march wound its way into Hamilton Square, Joe Rawlings and Leo McGree, who were at the front, looked at each other in astonishment. The police had barricaded off most of the Square. Large steel barriers had been erected, with a large contingent of unfriendly-looking policemen standing behind, so that it was impossible to get nearer to the Town Hall than

Brandon Street and Mortimer Street. Rawlings surmised that the police knew just a little too much about their plans. Whether or not the police did have informers inside their ranks is impossible to say, but given the constabulary's by now well-documented infiltration of the Communist Party and of the leadership of the NUWM at the time, it seems highly probable that someone — paid or otherwise — was passing on information to them about these activities. Not, of course, that it would have been too difficult for the police to guess their plans on this occasion. But later events were to suggest that Rawling's and McGree's suspicions of infiltration were well founded.

The presence of so many police in the Square, and their threatening attitude towards the unemployed, sparked off an immediate reaction. Anger spread, and there were calls to rush the barricades. But a strong detachment of police reinforcements soon deterred this challenge. The marchers also spotted that the main doors of the Town Hall had been closed, so the only remaining entrance was through a small and well-guarded side door.

As the Labour Councillors arrived at the Town Hall for their meeting, they were greeted by an outburst of cheering from the crowd, which by now had increased to over 5,000. But the cheering was soon followed by the first violence as the police moved into the crowd, intent on making an arrest. Shouts went up to leave alone the man they had picked on, but the constables paid no attention. Rather, they further antagonised the crowd by seizing some of the banners, claiming that they were being used in a threatening manner. With this, the unemployed marchers rushed the barriers, and a long line of police swayed under the force of the crowd, but somehow managed to remain upright. Tension was rising, and an otherwise peaceful demonstration was beginning to turn nasty.

In order to ease the situation, the Council decided to allow two deputations to enter the Town Hall: one from the NUWM; the other from the Dockers' Union. Rawlings, Cooper, Beatty, Roberts, and Barraskill comprised the NUWM deputation, while the dockers were represented by Nugent, Moffat, Quillan, Prince and Whatling. The council agreed that two speakers from each group should have ten minutes each to address the Council members.

The two groups were ushered into the imposing Council chamber and sat at a side table. They felt slightly uncomfortable in their casual dress: most of the Councillors wore smart, well-pressed suits with stiff white collars and highly-polished shoes.

George Nugent was the first speaker for the dockers. An active trade unionist, he was well accustomed to addressing meetings, and rose with the confidence of many years' experience. He told the Council that he was there as a representative of Birkenhead's trade unions. He outlined the protest of the town's unemployed against the exceptional hardships inflicted on them as a result of the Council's administration of the Means Test. He argued that it was within the power of the Council to give immediate consideration to these demands. In response, a few of the Councillors slowly shook their heads.

One of the principal points in dispute and one which those on the Means Test most bitterly resented, he continued, was the Council's chosen payment scale for a single person. 12 shillings a week simply was not enough. The rock-bottom budget for a single person living in the cheapest lodging house in town was 8d a night, or 4s 8d a week. Assuming that he had three meals a day, and took for each only a cup of tea and a cake, that would be 6d a day or 3s 6d a week, making a total expenditure of 8s 2d. That left just 3s 10d for maintenance, clothing, shoes, and so on. The unemployed were demonstrating not because they liked demonstrating, but because their stomachs compelled them to.

Labour Councillor, George Nugent continued by explaining that there were many older men on the demonstration who, because of the long periods of unemployment they had endured, and because of the shortage of food, were no longer fit to work. If they were suddenly set to work, he argued, they would face a considerable further risk to their health. (Indeed, there was much truth in this assertion, and when work commenced later on the Mersey Tunnel there was an abnormally high number of deaths from heart attacks.) At the end of his few minutes, George Nugent sat down to polite applause from the Council and friendly pats on the back from his colleagues.

Herbert Whatling spoke next, drawing attention to the sorry state of the building trade. There were over 1,000 building workers in Birkenhead walking the streets. The trade seemed to be the first one that was attacked by both municipal and national Governments whenever there was a call for savings. "To my certain knowledge," he claimed, "£50,000 worth of construction work could be started within the next fortnight." And he went on to point out how work on two schools had been halted. "The only housing scheme in hand at present is that on a few flats in Priory Street, yet there are 4,000 applicants on the housing list desperate for new accommodation."

Speaking for the NUWM, Joe Rawlings said that the

demonstrations held on 3rd August and 7th September, and now once again, reflected in no uncertain manner the massive determination of Birkenhead's unemployed to fight and struggle against the Council's application of the Means Test. He told the seated Councillors that if they cared to look through the windows, they would see the members of *his* class, the working class, held back by barriers and police.

"Let me warn you," he went on, "that if this continues much longer, barriers and policemen will not be able to hold the unemployed back. At the present moment they are beginning to feel so bitter about the viciousness which you are meting out to them that in a very short time from now, if the Council cannot see eye to eye with us in our demands, then it will be like hell let loose in this town, and in every other town and city throughout the country."

These were strong words which brought a predictably hostile reaction from a section of his audience, but which met with approval from some of the Labour members, as well as from his colleagues.

The first demand of the deputation, he continued, was for the abolition of the Means Test. They as a Town Council should do all they could to abolish it. He urged them to move a resolution referring to the misery and degradation of Birkenhead's working class and demanding that the National Government should abolish the Means Test. They should follow the example of Sheffield, Wigan, and the Vale of Leven, he argued, who had passed similar resolutions. Better still, he added, they could do as Durham had, and refuse to operate the Means Test, thereby defying the Minister of Labour. He further asked the Council to increase the unemployment benefit for a single man from 12s to 15s 3d, and that the Public Assistance Committee (PAC) should give relief to all able-bodied persons and bring the sons and daughters off the income of their parents; that the PAC should increase by 3s a week the relief to all able-bodied men, women and their dependents. He also demanded that boots and clothing should be supplied to the unemployed and their dependents along with one hundredweight of coal each week. Finally, work schemes such as building houses and schools, as well as programmes of road repairs, should be started immediately.

The next speaker was Mrs Barraskill. She spoke of the untold suffering that the working classes were enduring, and how they were not responsible for the system that had reduced them to a life of starvation and degradation. She appealed to the Councillors to bury their political differences. England was a

Christian nation, Birkenhead was a Christian borough, and she begged them as men and women of a great brotherhood to do all they could for their brothers and sisters outside. Between 1914 and 1918 they had gone to war to protect the interests of the property classes, for the working classes had nothing to lose. They had war memorials inscribed "Lest We Forget". How many members of the Town Council had forgotten? "The next time we fight", she added, "we will fight for our own interests and leave the property classes to fight for their interest themselves."

The Mayor thanked them for their contributions and the Council's discussion commenced. The delegation sat in an enforced silence, having been refused permission to participate in the debate.

Outside, the unemployed stood in steady drizzling rain, becoming more and more angry at the antics of the police. Inside the Town Hall the occasional roar from the demonstrators could be heard as tension increased between them and the police.

Alderman Mrs Mercer, opening the debate, voiced her support for the unemployed, adding that most people had come into some form of contact with the Means Test and therefore fully understood its implications. It was known, for instance, that a great deal of food was wasted in the country because people couldn't afford to buy it. That was not good economics. It was bad for people and bad for business. She believed that the Council should have no hesitation in sending a resolution to the Government.

Councillor Fletcher, speaking against the resolution, pointed out that things would be even worse if it wasn't for those administering the Means Test. He said that as a member of the Means Test committee he had broken the regulations time and time again. Three years ago the scale was 10s, and on the initiative of the Labour Party it had been raised to 12s. "The working classes are not the only people suffering. Many people wearing black coats are finding it very difficult to make ends meet and pay rents and taxes which the government is demanding." He concluded by pointing out that those wishing to abolish the Means Test should appeal to their MPs and not to the local Council.

The discussion continued around Mr McVey's resolution asking the government to abolish the Means Test, with all members, except Mr Fletcher, finally supporting it.

For: Aldermen Mrs Mercer, Miss Worrall, Mrs Grant, Aldermen Coulthard, Egan, Halligan, Herron, McVey, Nathan, Naylor, Vaughan, Messrs Allery, Birkett, Boyd, Barker, Caldwell,

Davies, Forsythe, Gossage, Hughes, Hurrell, McDonald, Miller, Milne, Noon, Platt, Poland, Power, Stephens and Van Grinsen. Against: Mr Fletcher.

The crowd outside was clearly becoming restless. As the shouting increased, those Councillors closest to the windows peered anxiously outside. A message, said to be from the Chief Constable, was passed to the meeting. It suggested that a deputation should go outside and tell the crowd what was happening. This was hurriedly agreed, and some of the unemployed's representatives volunteered to talk to the demonstrators.

Outside they found a dense crowd, far larger than on any of the previous days. The drizzling rain had turned to a heavy downpour, and most of the demonstrators were by now drenched to the skin. Standing on the Town Hall steps, Joe Rawlings told the crowd through a megaphone that the deputations had been in complete agreement. "This afternoon," he continued, "we can record a milestone in the history of the Birkenhead unemployed. In our statements to the Council, we laid it down in no uncertain fashion that you unemployed were prepared to fight, and barriers and police would not keep you back if our demands were not listened to." Loud cheers greeted his opening remarks.

"Our first demand has been agreed with only one against," he added.

"Give us his name!", shouted the crowd in response.

"The motion against the Means Test will be sent to the National Government from the Council," he said. The crowd roared its approval. Rawlings then asked them whether they wanted to wait to hear the Council's decision on the motion to increase the Means Test allowance or march on to the Haymarket. By a show of hands they agreed to wait.

Back inside the Council Chamber, Councillor Miller was on his feet moving the resolution, "That it be an instruction to the Public Assistance Committee to increase the scale for able-bodied unemployed persons to 15s 3d for single men and 13s 6d for single women."

He said that he need not stress the hardships that were taking place. That had already been expressed more than adequately by those speaking for the unemployed. In July the numbers on assistance were 363 single men and 57 single women at a cost of £3,500 or an extra penny rate. He believed that working class people would bear the increase in rates if they knew that distressed people in the town would be getting the benefit.

An argument broke out as to whether the Council had the right to instruct the PAC to give the increase, or take any decision on the matter whatsoever. Mr Power cited an instance at the clearing-house on the docks where a Birkenhead man was paid 12s benefit and was followed immediately by a Wallasey man who received 15s 3d. "We cannot justify such a discrepancy," he said.

Mr Baker consequently moved an amendment that the matter be referred back to the PAC for their consideration. He told the Council that he had recently sent a questionnaire to the various authorities and the following figures had been returned. Birkenhead paid 12s to a single man and 24s to a man and wife; Liverpool paid 12s and 20s respectively; Bootle paid 12s and 18s; Wallasey paid 10s and 18s. "It can be seen from the figures," he said, "that Birkenhead is not grinding the faces of the poor in the mire of poverty. I consider it my duty to the Council and ratepayers of Birkenhead to tell them of the serious and alarming increase in payment that has been given out in Poor Law relief. I have been informed by the Borough Treasurer that we are spending £1,000 a month over and above our estimates, and with the winter coming on I have not the slightest hesitation in saying that we will be coming to the Finance Committee to ask for a supplementary estimate of £20,000. And Mr Miller wants to add another two or three thousand pounds on top of that."

"There is another serious point," Baker continued. "Poor Law relief is being abused in some quarters and it is very difficult to detect. There are people earning money which they do not disclose by selling papers, acting as golf caddies, rag picking, selling football coupons, and so on, and claiming relief stating that they are destitute!" Loud hisses from the Labour benches greeted these remarks, but Mr Baker continued undeterred. "Recently, as one man was leaving the Relief Offices something dropped out of his pockets and it was found to be a betting slip containing the names of a lot of horses with sixpence marked on the side of each."

"Did they win?" asked Councillor Forsythe.

"This is a serious question," Mr Baker continued, adding that another man had £150 in his possession, all of which had been spent in three months. He told the committee a lot of lies and they found out that it had been spent on drinking and gambling, and yet he expected the ratepayers to support his wife and children. There was an alarming number of couples getting married, he continued, and then coming to the PAC the next day seeking relief. With not a penny in the world, they got married and threw themselves on the PAC. Parents were sending boys and girls of only fourteen years of age to them seeking relief, while some of their investigators called on single men living together and found that they were not up by 10.30 am. The committee had set aside a certain sum for boots, many of which had been exchanged or had found their way to the pawn shop. There were also people coming from Canada and America, settling with friends in Birkenhead, and then approaching the PAC for relief.

·When it was put to the vote, Mr Baker's amendment was carried by 22 votes to 18.

For: Aldermen Solly, Messrs Baker, Baxter, Boyd, Bullock, Caldwell, G.Davies, Dr.Dawson, Furnival, Gaskell, Gossage, Hodgkinson, Hughes, Hurrell, McDonald, McWilliam, Merritt, Milne, Nottingham, Staples, Van Grinsen and Miss Worrall.

Against: Aldermen Coulthard, Egan, Halligan, Herron, McVey, Mrs Mercer, Nathan, Naylor, Vaughan, Messrs Allery, Cargill, W Davies, Forsythe, Miller, Noon, Platt, Poland and Power.

Having decided to refer the matter to the PAC, the meeting then ended and the Council rose.

Joe Rawlings walked outside to the top of the Town Hall steps. It was late in the evening and, although the rain had now stopped, it was still damp and windy. He told the waiting crowd, who by now must have been both hungry and cold, that the reactionary Conservative Town Council had sat from 5 pm until 8 pm, and the only thing they had done in the interest of the unemployed had been to move a resolution of protest to the National Government against the Means Test. The 15s 3d matter was referred back to the General Purposes Committee of the PAC. He was clearly dispirited.

He said, "From this night the unemployed must organise still larger demonstrations. They have got to refuse in no uncertain way to accept a starvation allowance from the Council and the National Government. We have had a talk with the dockers' deputation, and they have agreed that we must discuss the matter of organising a demonstration to the PAC under rank and file control."

Councillor Nugent then asked if he could speak. He told the crowd that he and his colleagues regarded the Council's decision as entirely unsatisfactory. He suggested that they march in orderly fashion to the Park Entrance where they would be told in detail about the Council's proceedings.

The crowd agreed, and as they moved off and out of Hamilton Square they began chanting "We want work!" At the Park Entrance wives, children and some who were in work assembled to greet them. It was getting dark, but this had not deterred a large crowd from gathering. They were told that the PAC would be meeting on Thursday and that it was essential to organise a mass demonstration. The chairman said that if they had had 2,000 dockers they could have swept aside the barriers, invaded the Town Hall, and waited until the Council had met their demands.

As the crowd dispersed into the cold autumn night, Joe Rawlings had a final word with his colleagues. They would meet early the next day and make arrangements for their demonstration. It had to be impressive, he insisted.

CHAPTER SIX

"Birkenhead's Communistic Reign of Terror"

"If I had to live in conditions like that I would be a revolutionary myself."
King George V

Bedraggled after their damp vigil outside the Town Hall, the unemployed who had been at the demonstration spent the best part of Wednesday drying out.[1] For most of them it had been a tiring and frustrating day with little to show at the end of it. But it had not defeated their resolve. The political activists in their ranks were busy planning how to make the next demonstration even more impressive. In order to bring home their case to the council, it was vital to bring as many unemployed people on to the streets as possible. A poor turnout would only play into the hands of their Conservative opponents. The message now had to go out to all trade unionists that, if they could afford the time off, they should join the demonstration planned for the next day. The chalkers were out early covering the town, while down at the Labour Exchange the message was passed around.

And they did a good job. Joe Rawlings could hardly believe the numbers when he arrived at the Park Entrance. Even before 2 pm, the square was jammed. By 2.30 pm it was estimated that more than 15,000 people were ready to march. It was a mass of colour. As the procession moved off, the hurriedly-made banners were raised high. The crowd stretched for almost a mile, so that when those at the front had reached the Public Assistance Office, those at the rear had only just left the park. Birkenhead had not seen the likes of this before, and the reporter from the *Birkenhead News* who was following the demonstration vividly caught the atmosphere[2]:

> "The procession proceeded in more or less orderly fashion, five and six deep. In the main, it was a peaceful gathering, if a motley one. Men in ragged clothing and worn out shoes; men with clothes faded yet neatly pressed, and shoes brightly polished; here and there an upright, professional-looking man; men with

washed overalls that had not known the grime of the shipyards for months; old men with whitewashed hair and bent shoulders; young boys but shortly out of school; each one ready to shout in the chorus of 'Struggle or Starve' and 'Down with the Means Test'."

The procession wound its way down Conway Street and into Argyle Street towards the Public Assistance Office where the PAC committee was meeting. So big was the crowd that only about 8,000 of them were able to pack themselves into the street outside the office. The other 10,000 crammed into Conway Street, hoping to catch a glimpse of what was happening ahead.

The police were taking no chances. All leave had been cancelled, and it seemed that the entire Birkenhead force was on duty that day in the vicinity of the PAC offices. All the entrances were well guarded by a mass of blue uniforms, but even they were clearly having trouble keeping the demonstrators at bay. One surge forward and the line of blue almost gave way; a fresh detachment was sent for in order to hold ranks. Realising that they must eventually lose the struggle, the Chief Constable agreed to allow a deputation to enter the building to put its points to the Public Assistance Committee.

As they talked inside, the crowd in the street grew restless. Insults and shouts of "blackleg" were hurled at some of the men peering through the windows of the neighbouring billiard hall. After about an hour of waiting, the crowd suddenly swept forward towards the entrance. The police drew their batons and struggled to push back the surging mass. Just as it seemed inevitable that the crowd would storm into the entrance, another 20 or 30 policemen appeared from inside the building where they had been waiting for such a moment. Gradually, the unemployed demonstrators were forced back, but not before some damage had been done. One man aimed a blow at a constable and received one in return, knocking him backwards into the angry crowd. The police deliberately broke a banner, provoking a storm of protest.

Inside the offices, in one of the small committee rooms, the Public Assistance Committee sat around a square oak table, listening to the noise outside. When the chairman, Councillor Baker, began the meeting by informing them that he had agreed to allow a deputation into the building, it brought a howl of complaint from some of the Conservative members. "They have no legal right to be in the building, let alone this meeting," shouted Councillor Fletcher. They were nothing but a rabble, and could not force their views onto other people simply by their numbers and tactics. He was having none of it and, along with Councillor Baxter and the Reverend McPherson, walked out of the meeting.

Against a background of noise and confusion, Councillor Baker invited the deputation, led by Joe Rawlings and including two women, to put their points to the meeting. There was little the committee could do, they were told, except to place the demands for abolition of the Means Test and for increased unemployment benefits before the full committee at their next meeting on Monday.

Rawlings reacted angrily. "We're being fobbed off yet again," he stormed. "All you ever decide is to discuss it at the next meeting." With that, the deputation marched out.

Rawlings' reappearance with his colleagues at the entrance to the offices brought an instant cheer from the demonstrators. Squeezing past the cordon of policemen, he told the crowd, "We've got nowhere again. It's the same old story, the same old excuses." And he reminded the huge crowd of Councillor Baker's remarks on Tuesday, that the unemployed only wasted their time at midweek football matches and in breeding expensive racing dogs. "Make him come out and apologise," someone yelled. Seizing on the remark, Rawlings said he would do just that. "I'll go in there now and make him apologise to you." As he turned to re-enter the building, a roar of approval went up.

Ten minutes later he was back — alone. "Where's Baker?, " screamed the crowd, "We want him."

"He's hiding behind locked doors," replied Rawlings. "He won't come out to apologise to you!"

Leo McGree then stepped onto the wooden box, which somebody had produced, and spoke to the crowd. He said that they should all march, in an orderly manner, back to the Park Entrance, and plan a further demonstration for Monday. He continued, "We must fight to the end. On Monday the Means Test must be a thing of the past in Birkenhead."

Appearing dispirited at the lack of results, the crowd nevertheless agreed to McGree's proposal and trudged through the streets once again towards the Park. The police Chief heaved a sigh of relief, and sent only a small band of his men to accompany the marchers.

As the demonstration approached Oxton Road, however, there were cries of "We want to go to Baker's house", and the crowd began to get excited. Joe Rawlings said that it would be a foolish thing to do, but the "agents provocateurs", as he later called them, only carried on encouraging and exciting the marchers. Eventually, some 2,000 protesters broke free from the main body of the march and stormed up Woodchurch Road towards Councillor Baker's smart house in Bryanston Road. By now Baker was the focus for all their abuse and insults. If anyone was to blame for their predicament, it was Baker, they reckoned. There was no way of holding back their anger. Even Rawlings and McGree had joined them.

When this second crowd reached Councillor Baker's house, they surged around it,challenging him to come out. Rawlings walked up the path to the front door, peered through the curtains, and then knocked. Baker's son answered the door and told him that his father was out at a function in town. As Rawlings walked back down the path and closed the gate, he saw half a dozen police vans turning into the street. What happened next is described by the reporter from the *Birkenhead News*[3].

"About 15 or 20 policemen jumped out of the vans and immediately cleared a space in front of the house. They then formed up in line, drew their batons, and the order was given to charge. They charged amid a hail of stones, brickbats and plant pots taken from neighbouring gardens, and the mob fled in all directions, jumping over garden walls, hiding in doorways and running down passages at the sides of houses. The police struck out right and left and scores of men went down, dragging down others who stumbled in their headlong flight. Scores of people lay about the roadway, many with their heads cut open, groaning with the pain."

This smaller crowd had been caught in a trap, the narrow road hampering all their hopes of escape. "We were brutally beaten by the police," said Rawlings. "They went straight into the crowd and smashed the hell out of them. They had specially made batons, knocking me and the others all over the place. It wasn't the unemployed who provoked what was to follow, it was the police." This time, the *Birkenhead News* concurred[4]:

"Batons were wielded to good effect by the police, who scattered the flying ranks of the mob in all directions, leaving about fifty of them screaming and shouting on the road."

The injured were taken by ambulance to the General Hospital. Those who escaped rushed down to the Park Entrance to tell the other crowd, who by this time were listening to speeches from some Labour Councillors. The news rapidly spread throughout the town, turning the orderly, unemployed demonstrators into a riotous mob. It was the spark that was to ignite a series of events that would be remembered for years to come.

That evening, as darkness fell, some of the unemployed went on a rampage that lasted for more than four days. They were angry and hungry; they had had enough of the Council's fudging and demanded action. If the Council wouldn't act, then they would.

One group of 30 or so swept down Grange Road, the town's main shopping centre, and began smashing windows and looting shops, taking shoes, clothes, and furniture from the shattered shop fronts. The windows of the Queen's Hotel, next to the Gaumont Cinema at Park Entrance, were smashed, and bottles of whisky and gin stolen. The huge glass windows of Herron's motor-car salesroom, situated opposite, were also smashed, showering glass over the pavement and road. In the Price Street area looting took place on a large scale, with grocery shops suffering the most.

The police were by now only making things worse by their aggressive approach. They had suffered casualties in the initial skirmishes outside Councillor Baker's house, and appeared to be out for revenge. It was in the early evening when the police moved in to disperse the crowd at Park Entrance that the serious violence began.

Angered by this seemingly gratuitous attack on people doing little except discussing in small groups the events of the day, some of the unemployed retaliated fiercely. Running battles broke out as the police drew their truncheons and charged across the square. Some people managed to break off the iron spikes on the railings around the park, and together with bricks these were used as missiles to hurl at the police.

The *Birkenhead News*[5] reported that "pandemonium was let loose at the Park Entrance where rioters wrenched the spikes from the park railings and hurled them at the police, several of whom received bad injuries." Such an unexpected retaliation by the unemployed only exacerbated the bad behaviour of the police.

Later in the evening, a large mob made off for Councillor Fletcher's house in Borough Road, intent on attacking it. They were quickly dispersed by a contingent of policemen long before they got anywhere near.

A speaker at the Park Entrance paraded an injured old man and addressed the growing crowd. "This is what the police have done tonight," he told them. "On Monday I want you all to come with weapons, and if the police try to interfere with us, we will not be responsible."

Elsewhere in the town Joe Rawlings was whipping up feelings. He told a crowd at the market place, "On Monday afternoon all the working classes will have to be in the streets of this town to demonstrate. We don't want 10,000, but 20,000 or 50,000. We will have to be organised into a regiment, and we will march as we marched in 1914." To cheers from the crowd he added, "We will march feeling that we are going to attack, and that attack is our best form of defence. Dawson (the Chief Constable) and his thugs won't do anything then, and if he sends to Liverpool for police he will be a bit unlucky because our fellow workers are organising a mass demonstration to keep them busy." Little did Joe Rawlings know that this would be his last speech for some time.

Throughout the night of Thursday 15th September, and into the early hours of Friday, the violence continued, with both sides finding safety in numbers. The Chief Constable, Captain Dawson, who was being urged by his officers to take a tough line, had a meeting with the Mayor and the Town Clerk at the Central Police Station. Eight police officers had been reported injured, along with 37 civilians, including four women. Police injuries were generally to the shoulders and legs, while civilian casualties included 16 with head wounds as a result of baton charges and four fractures of the skull.

In an editorial the following day, the *Birkenhead News*[6] condemned those who had perpetrated so much violence:

> "The unemployed in the Borough should realise that they will not advance their own interest by giving way to anger and yielding to the counsel of extremists . . . if the Birkenhead Committee ventured to follow the example of Lincoln and Durham and refused to apply the Means Test, the Government, unless they altered their policy, would almost certainly send down their officials who would carry on the work, with far less consideration than up to the present time has been shown . . . The PAC spends £1,000 per week above their estimates. The good name of Birkenhead should not be dragged down by acts of violent disorder."

After midnight on Thursday, the disturbances receded as police reinforcements moved into the town. Large groups of policemen patrolled the main areas of trouble in Price Street, Grange Road, and the Park Entrance. By now the streets were deserted. Only an occasional workman repairing a shop front was to be seen.

Six arrests had been made in the course of that Thursday. The men arrested were Chistopher May (who had also been arrested on Tuesday outside the Town Hall), George Briggs, John Tighe, John Prescott, Arthur Smith, and William McCulloch. They all appeared in court the following day, where bail was refused and they were remanded in custody for one week.

Friday passed off with surprisingly few disturbances. Perhaps the battles of the previous evening had stunned the demonstrators, or maybe they were counting the cost of their injuries. Certainly, Birkenhead was buzzing with talk of the previous night's fights, even though daylight threw a different perspective on the struggles. By morning the police were out in force again, determined to stamp out any trouble while, unknown to the ranks of the unemployed, the Chief Constable was applying for warrants before the local magistrates to arrest all the known ringleaders.

The warrants were agreed, and took effect from midnight on Friday. In the early hours of Saturday morning a carefully planned police operation began.

Joe Rawlings, after attending a meeting that Friday evening, went to bed about midnight. He was sound asleep when the police vans turned into Hampden Road in Higher Tranmere. Out jumped a dozen policemen; some of them began hammering on his door, while the others ran round the back to cut off any escape route. Joe was taken by surprise. He had not expected the police suddenly to descend on him, and he was astonished when he opened the door to find a group of police officers standing outside. He was arrested and taken down to the Bridewell. That night seven of Birkenhead's leading political activists were arrested and taken into custody. Like Joe Rawlings, they were all apprehended in the early hours.

The following morning they appeared in court before Alderman Mrs Mercer and Mr Halsall, charged that on Thursday, "with divers other persons to the number of several hundreds, they unlawfully and riotously assembled and made a great riot to the terror and alarm of His Majesty's subjects and against the police." No members of the public were allowed into the heavily guarded court. Outside, policemen patrolled the streets.

Prosecuting on behalf of the Chief Constable, the Town Clerk described Thursday's demonstration outside the Public Assistance Offices, and how the unemployed had marched down Grange Road before turning their attention to Councillor Baker's home. He then described the later confrontation in Bryanston Road. Despite the seven defendants' pleas of innocence, they were all remanded in custody for a week. Joe Rawlings and his fellow prisoners were escorted back to the cells, well away from the crisis that was about to erupt on the streets of Birkenhead.

Saturday afternoon was strangely peaceful. There were few signs that, only 48 hours earlier, the town had been caught up in a wave of violence which the *Birkenhead News* had headlined as "Birkenhead's Communistic Reign of Terror". Some shop windows were still boarded up, while others were being repaired hurriedly. But down Grange Road, families were out as usual doing the Saturday shopping, with the women standing around the market stalls, haggling over the price of the weekly groceries in the hope of some late afternoon bargains.

There were few disturbances that day until the evening. Then the police broke up the NUWM's weekly meeting at the Haymarket. Meanwhile, down the road, the fascists were allowed to gather without disturbance, and even received police protection! The police gave no reason for dispersing the NUWM's meeting, where there had been no hint of trouble. In acting as they did, the police generated further resentment amongst the unemployed who, as they went off towards the Park Entrance, spoke of revenge. A crowd quickly began to gather near the Park Entrance — always a focal point on a Saturday evening — but even more so on this particular weekend. Here the unemployed felt more secure in their strength of numbers, and they regarded the area as their own territory. But before long the police moved in and pushed the crowd away from the square where they could so easily congregate in large numbers. More than a hundred policemen burst out of their vans and poured into the square, scattering people in all directions. Bricks and other missiles rained down on the police as the battle began. Some of the rioters had chisels and hammers and broke off the remaining spikes from the park railings to use as weapons. In the streets around the Park Entrance, whenever a body of policemen advanced, the unemployed vanished into the houses and, under the cover of darkness, pelted the police with stones and bricks from upstairs windows. From some of the bedroom windows, women threw crockery down on the heads of the police. And immediately the police detachment had passed by, the rioters returned to the streets. One police patrol was trapped down a blind alley, and attacked by a crowd of more than 500. Wielding their batons, they struggled grimly to escape serious injury.

Lieutenant-Colonel John Sandeman Allen, Conservative Member of Parliament for Birkenhead West, reacted predictably to the violence[7]:

"From what I have gathered this morning it seems that a lot of young hooligan elements, youths of about 20 years of age who do not even belong to Birkenhead, took an active part in the trouble. I believe that the whole thing is organised by Liverpool Communists with the aid of Birkenhead Communists."

He added, somewhat graciously:

". . . the general mass of genuine unemployed are sober, self-sacrificing, decent people who know that rioting and revolution such as occurred yesterday are going to do infinitely more harm than anything else. In my opinion the flabby lack of leadership in the Socialist Party has largely contributed to this state of affairs."

The town's other Member of Parliament, Graham White, a Liberal, said little. By now, *The Times* had been alerted to events in Birkenhead. Their report said[8]:

"During what amounted to a series of pitched battles between the mob and the police, nine officers and seven other persons were taken to hospital . . . The police tried to break up the mob, but were met with a rain of bottles, stones, lumps of lead, hammer-heads, and other missiles . . . Wherever the police were seen sweeping up a street the rioters disappeared into houses, from the windows of which women threw all kinds of missiles . . . In one street the manhole cover of a sewer was lifted and a wire rope stretched across the street. A number of police fell over this . . . One of the motor omnibuses conveying police reinforcements had all its windows broken."

In Back St Anne Street a wall was demolished in order to provide ammunition to throw at the police. Trip wires were stretched across the road to await mounted policemen. Manhole covers were removed to furnish a trap for unwary foot patrols. When the gas lamps were broken the whole area was plunged into total darkness.

Fourteen shops were smashed and looted in Price Street alone. The rioters ransacked one particular barber's shop patronised by policemen. Similarly, a pub at the corner of Victoria Street and Beckwith Street, which was a regular drinking haunt for policemen, was also smashed. Those that did it then helped themselves to a free drink.

Police vans arriving back at the Central Police Station often had smashed windscreens and bore the marks made by bricks thrown at them. The rioting continued throughout Saturday night, and the Chief Constable passed his requests for reinforcements further afield beyond Liverpool.

Casualties on both sides were heavy, with a stream of injured people arriving for treatment at the General Hospital. Many of those from the ranks of the unemployed who were injured were afraid to go to hospital, fearing that it would only lead to arrest. But those who were seriously injured had to be taken there for treatment. Over the weekend 65 people were treated at the General, arising from the riot — of these, 45 were civilians and 20 were policemen.

On Sunday, the Chief Constable's reinforcements arrived in Birkenhead. They came not only from across the Mersey, but from as far away as Birmingham and Chester. In a show of strength, Captain Dawson marched his forces in military columns through the town, warning that any further attacks that day would be met with solid resistance. He told the crowd[9]:

"The police may be forced to take similar steps to what were taken yesterday, and there will be grave risk of injury to innocent persons."

The unemployed looked on, but were not impressed. As one ferry-boat load of police from Liverpool approached Woodside Pier, they threw stones at the boat, making it impossible for the ferry to dock. In the end the ferry-boat had to turn around and go back to Liverpool, and the police used the underground railway instead.

After a lull on Sunday lasting most of the daytime hours, serious rioting returned to Birkenhead's streets that evening. Even with their reinforcements, the police could not contain the situation. Around Conway Street and the docks, the working-class streets of back-to-back terraced houses had become virtual no-go areas for the police, though they battled to gain a foothold. Then, in a determined effort to seize control, the police began to terrorize the residents. They descended on the area in lorry loads, blocking off entrances and invading private homes, often coming through the back doors which were usually unlocked. They claimed that they were searching for goods from the shops that had been looted. Their invasion led to many allegations of brutality against them.

One such charge came from Mrs Davin, wife of an ex-serviceman invalided out of the army.[10]

"The worst night of all was Sunday night, 18th September, about 1.30am. We were fast asleep in bed at Morpeth Buildings, having had no sleep the two previous nights and my husband was very poorly. My old mother, 68 and paralysed, could not sleep. She was so terrified. I have five children, a daughter 19, one 15, a son 17, one of 12, and one 6. Suddenly my old mother screeched. She is unable to speak. We were all wakened at the sound of heavy motor vehicles, which turned out to be Black Marias. Lights in the houses were lit, windows opened to see what was going on. Policemen bawled out, 'Lights out!,' and 'Pull up those . . . windows.' Hordes of police came rushing up the stairs, doors were smashed in, the screams of women and children were terrible. We could hear the thuds of the blows from the batons. Presently our doors were bashed by heavy instruments. My husband got out of bed and, without waiting to put his trousers on, unlocked the door. As he did so, 12 police rushed into the room, knocking him to the floor, his poor head being split open, kicking him as he lay there. We were all in our night-clothes. The language of the police was terrible. I tried to prevent them hitting my husband. Then they commenced to baton me all over the arms and body. As they hit me and my Jim, the children and I were screaming, and the police shouted 'Shut up, you parish-fed bastards!'."

Mrs Sullivan, who lived close to the Park Entrance, also recalled the policemen's tactics[11]:

"On Sunday, the night after the raid, I and my husband were in bed, and my younger brother, 17 years of age, and older brother were in another room. We were awakened by the screams and noise, but I was too terrified to move. One of my brothers opened the door, and the police pounced on him, batoning him right and left. They then set about the younger brother as he lay in bed; he had been working and would not take part in the recent demonstration. Ten officers came back and searched my house just as I was going back to bed. The door lock was smashed and they just walked in as I was undressing. I said, 'What have you come back for? Can't you see my condition — have you no sense of shame?' They replied, 'you have some loot here', and they then commenced to search the room."

Other claims were listed later, of husbands and sons beaten up in their own homes, and of furniture smashed by the police. The constables also ran amock down back streets, smashing windows with their truncheons as they went. While his officers were terrorizing the area, the Chief Constable gave further consideration to bringing in the army. He had 350 police reinforcements from Liverpool and 500 from Birmingham, and he now decided to put Chester Barracks on alert.

Serious allegations about police conduct were repeated in court when the 31 people arrested over the weekend came up before the bench. In court the Chief Constable promised to initiate an inquiry into the allegations but, if such an inquiry was ever made, its findings were never published.

By midnight on Sunday, thousands of pounds worth of damage had been done, and a total of 44 men were in police custody. Rows of shops stood smashed and looted, homes had been damaged, walls demolished, and bricks lay strewn in the roads.

Asked about the demonstration proposed for the following day, Captain Dawson, the Chief Constable, warned[12]:

> "This is a direct challenge to law and order in Birkenhead and the people concerned will be held responsible for any misguided action they choose to take."

CHAPTER SEVEN

An Unexpected Victory

"You'll get pie in the sky when you die."
Joe Hill

Monday 19th September[1] was to be an important day for
Birkenhead's thousands of unemployed and their families. After
a weekend of extensive rioting, they were in no mood for back-
peddling or fudging by the Public Assistance Committee. The
PAC knew this; so did the Conservative Council and the Chief
Constable. For their part, the unemployed knew that they had to
keep up the pressure. This time Joe Rawlings wasn't there to
advise them. Leo McGree had been arrested in Liverpool and was
in detention, accused of inciting a riot. Other known members of
the Communist Party had been seized by the police in dawn
swoops. But there were still some political activists able to
encourage and organise the day's demonstration.

Captain Dawson was very worried. As he toured the riot-torn
streets and viewed the smashed buildings, barricades, broken
windows, and the bottles and bricks used as missiles, he knew
that it might be even worse by tomorrow. What he didn't know
was how much longer he could hold out before calling in the
army. He remembered the last time the troops had been called on
to the streets of Birkenhead, during the 1926 General Strike. The
lesson of that experience was that soldiers patrolling the town
would only lead to further problems. In 1919, during the police
strike, troops had been called out in Birkenhead to maintain law
and order, as they had during the 1911 dock strike. Troops, he
surmised, might not be new to the streets of Birkenhead, but they
would be a pointer to the outside world that law and order had
truly broken down on Captain Dawson's patch.

Monday began with the 31 arrested men appearing at the
Borough Police Court before Alderman Marsh, Mr Fletcher and
Mr Byrne. Strict security was in force outside the court. The
public were not allowed inside, and a large detachment of

mounted police patrolled the street, keeping everyone on the move. Before the court were:

James Frame (aged 45) of Brook Place,
James Cherry (25) of St Anne Street,
William McDonald (28) of Church Street,
John Cladwell (58) of Brook Street,
Francis Price (25) of Formby Street,
Stanley Lockenby (20) of Conway Street,
Reuben Little (22) of Seacombe,
John Cross (29) of Brook Street,
Robert McKay (16) of Goodwin Avenue,
Terence Flynn (16) of Hoylake Road,
John Price (43) of Gorsey Crescent, Wallasey,
Samuel Griffiths (23) of Upper Beckwith Street,
John Carruthers of Birch Avenue,
Albert Branscombe (46) of Rodney Street,
James Waring (38) of Garfield Place,
John Smith (33) of Brook Street,
Paul Davin (47) of Morpeth Buildings,
Thomas Sullivan (30) of Morpeth Buildings,
George Carroll (18) of Morpeth Buildings,
Thomas Fallon (35) of Morpeth Buildings,
Henry Forrester (47) of Morpeth Buildings,
Harry Forrester (22) of Morpeth Buildings,
James Forrester (18) of Morpeth Buildings,
Joseph Kenna (26) of Morpeth Buildings,
William Kenna (32) of Morpeth Buildings,
Thomas Lewis (32) of Price Street,
William Ashworth of St Paul's Road,
John Bordley (29) of Evelyn Avenue.

The addresses clearly showed that Morpeth Buildings had been a prime target of police raids.

One by one the defendants entered the dock, displaying a remarkable procession of bandaged heads, black eyes, swollen lips, and a number of other visible injuries.

The first defendant, James Frame, had been arrested for using bad language, but on arrival at the police station was found to have two stones in his pocket. Another defendant, James Waring, was accused along with John Smith of stealing cigarettes from a shop which had been broken into and looted. Both pleaded not guilty, swearing that they had not had any cigarettes in their pockets until the police had put them there after they had arrived at the police station. A number of other defendants accused the police of planting things on them, particularly those charged with possessing dangerous weapons. Generally, these dangerous weapons were bricks. A number of others were accused of throwing bricks at the police and causing injury. Most of the accused pleaded not guilty and, with bail refused in all cases, the 31 men were remanded and left the dock to spend another week in custody.

In contrast to previous occasions, this time the unemployed did not assemble at the Park Entrance. The police had already cordoned off the square, and with road blocks erected in the neighbouring streets, they had made it abundantly clear that they were not going to allow any march through the town. Nor were there enough activists still free who could organise such a march. Instead, the word went round to congregate outside the PAC offices at 4.30pm.

By late afternoon the autumn sun was setting, and a slight chill was blowing up from the Mersey. The size of the crowd which had gathered early outside the PAC office surprised even the Chief Constable. He estimated that more than 20,000 people were crammed into the streets around the office. Unemployed men had been joined by their wives, while shipyard workers from Cammell Laird had also downed tools to join in. Argyle street was a mass of faces and banners. Nobody in Birkenhead could recall so many gathered in one place before.

Long after 4.30pm, people continued to join the demonstration as those in work finished their shifts and came to stand alongside the unemployed. Hundreds of police patrolled the streets in an attempt to keep order, while plain-clothed detectives mingled with the crowd. Initially the atmosphere was tense as the police attempted to keep people on the move but, realising the hopelessness of their task, the constables eventually gave up and resigned themselves to supervising the stationary mass.

Shortly after the meeting of the Public Assistance Committee had started, a deputation was allowed inside the PAC offices. The Committee had agreed to receive a deputation from the Birkenhead branch of the NUWM. At first it seemed that the members of the deputation were destined to sit through another depressing session, as resolutions were re-submitted and left to lie on the table once more. When success finally came, it happened unexpectedly and almost casually. Item 39 on the agenda proposed that the weekly scale of relief for able-bodied single men be increased from 12s to 15s 3d, and for single women to 13s 6d. It was proposed and agreed almost without discussion, and submitted for ratification to the next Council meeting. The members of the NUWM deputation were informed that, having been passed by the PAC, the Council's approval of the increases was assured.

A genuine victory had been won. The increases would help to make life significantly easier for those without work. The rise worked out at more than 25 per cent and represented a considerable improvement. At the PAC meeting it was also announced that work schemes costing £170,000 would be introduced that winter to help alleviate unemployment, and this would mean jobs for many. In addition, the Council was committed to lobbying the Government for an end to the Means Test.

Not that these advances represented total victory. Some of the requests made on behalf of the town's unemployed had been firmly rejected by the PAC, and many of the activists in the NUWM remained in detention. Had they been free and believed that more could be done, then the campaign might well have continued. Nevertheless, it was a victory which a fortnight earlier had seemed inconceivable.

The NUWM deputation could barely wait to leave the meeting and relate the news to the thousands outside. When they walked out through the office door, their smiles instantly revealed that a victory had been won. It was 6.30pm, and the crowd was as large as ever. The announcement of the increase in unemployment benefit brought a loud cheer. People threw their hats in the air and waved their banners. Word of their triumph rapidly spread through the town, helped on by notices posted up in shop windows and pubs.

Captain Dawson, watching from inside the PAC offices, heaved a sigh of relief. He knew that, for the time being at least, it would put an end to the demonstrations and fighting.

That evening the police went off duty exhausted by the confrontations of recent days, while some of those on public assistance celebrated their forthcoming rises. Local Council workers had been out that day clearing up the debris. But the broken-down walls and dismembered railings around the park remained for some years to come as a legacy of a depressing period in Birkenhead's history.

CHAPTER EIGHT
The Trial

"No morality can be founded on authority, even if the authority is divine."
A.J. Ayer

On Tuesday 25th October 1932[1], in the old Roman city of Chester, some 15 miles from Birkenhead, the trial began of the seven ringleaders arrested in the early hours of 21st September. They appeared before Mr Justice Charles, charged with creating a disturbance outside the home of Councillor Baker in Bryanston Road, Birkenhead. The seven were: Joseph Rawlings (aged 38), Christopher May (19), John McAllister (47), William McBeth (40), Sidney Greenwood (20), George Williams (29), Benjamin Anderson (32), Richard Murphy (20), John Tighe (49), and George Biggs.

Inspector Williams told the court what, in the view of the police, had taken place outside Mr Baker's house. He said that the crowd had deliberately gone to Mr Baker's house with the intention of breaking into it. He was convinced that had the police not taken the action which they did, the rioters would have smashed their way in, endangering the lives of the occupants. He insisted that the police had used their batons for only two or three minutes, and that the police themselves had been stoned continuously by the rioters.

When his turn came to speak, Joe Rawlings was adamant that the demonstration in Bryanston Road had been a peaceful one and that the police, quite unprovoked, had drawn their batons and attacked the crowd. He said that a deputation of eight, including himself and two women, had gone to the door of Baker's house. When they were told that Councillor Baker was not in, he had stood on the garden wall and told the crowd, "I am told that Baker is not in. Let us march back." He went on, "As soon as I had finished, I noticed that the police were using their batons in a brutal fashion on the unemployed." The judge immediately interrupted, telling him, "We don't want any propaganda here. We know there were some thousands of people and six police. We don't want any talk of brutality and all that when there were only six police."

Turning to the defence counsel, Mr Elsden, the judge added that if Rawlings attempted to make anything like propaganda speeches again, he would go back to the dock and give no further evidence. But Joe Rawlings insisted that there was no riot, with no missiles thrown, and that the police attack had been unprovoked.

Sidney Greenwood appeared in the witness box next. He told the Court that he was born in London and had come to Birkenhead when he was seven years old. He had a wife and three children, and had been unemployed for the past 20 months. As an unemployed husband and father he received 29s 3d transitional benefit. He admitted that he had been a member of the Communist Party for some considerable time and that, along with Rawlings, he had been responsible for organising the demonstrations. He also admitted that he had signed the letter to the Lord Mayor, although he was not a member of the National Unemployed Workers' Movement. Accused of inciting the crowd and throwing missiles, he denied both charges.

William McBeth told the court that he was born in Barrow and that, after some fruitless years in the United States, he had stowed away on a ship back to Glasgow in 1931. He too was unemployed, but not in receipt of any transitional benefit. He was actively connected with the Communist Party and had helped to organise the demonstrations, but he claimed that he had not been within half a mile of the demonstration at Councillor Baker's house.

George Williams said that he was a member of the Communist Party and that he had been involved in the demonstrations. He came from Fishguard in South Wales, and had been without work for three years. He estimated that the crowd outside the PAC offices had been in the region of 15 to 20,000, but that there were no more than 2,000 in Bryanston Road. The judge emphasised that the majority of the crowd had not joined this "adventure" to Baker's house. Williams added that he thought the crowd had been perfectly law-abiding the whole time.

When John McAllister went into the witness box, he claimed that he had been struck on the head and the back by a police baton while he was standing, arms folded, at the back of the crowd in Bryanston Road.

"Where were you born?" asked the judge.

"I don't know," replied McAllister.

"I dare say he has been told he was born in Ireland," interrupted the prosecuting counsel, in an obvious attempt to link the Birkenhead incidents with the Irish.

McAllister replied pointedly, "My mother did happen to be an Irish woman. One man's mother is born in one country, another man's in another, and that's all there is in nationality . . . I never asked to come into the world but I am here."

He said that he had been a pacifist all his life, believing that the world hit people hard enough without them hitting one another. He added that he was going on the demonstration for a long walk, like a good soldier. It was unfortunate that he mentioned the word "soldier", as the prosecuting counsel seized upon it. "Are you putting yourself forward as a good soldier or a good pacifist?" he demanded.

"A good soldier is a good humane man," replied McAllister. "When I say soldier I don't mean a man who pulls off his coat and challenges everybody in the street. The thing that pulls its coat off in the street isn't a man at all but is changed into a lower animal . . . I may say, seeing as you are lacking a bit, that it is the hardest job in the world to get people to understand one another. If you don't understand me properly, that is not my fault. It is entirely yours. I am neither a mental acrobat nor a prophet."

As he was dismissed from the witness box, his supporters in the court smiled in sympathy with his remarks. But such sentiments were hardly likely to win much sympathy from the judge.

Benjamin Anderson, the prosecution alleged, was not one of the leaders of the demonstration. Rather, he had gone along "just for a pastime," and claimed that the crowd had been perfectly orderly outside the house. But the judge was having none of this. "If it was so perfectly orderly," he inquired, "why should Mr Baker's son need to call the police for assistance?"

George Briggs, a native of Birkenhead, told the court that he had served for six years in the Cheshire Regiment and the Royal Army Medical Corps during the First World War, and that he had been demobbed in 1919. In recent years he had only been able to find casual employment, and at the time of his arrest he was receiving unemployment benefit of £1 11s 3d a week. The court was told that he was thought to be a member of the Communist Party. Defence counsel questioned why this should be of importance to the trial, but the judge intervened to say that he didn't sentence people because they were members of the Communist Party.

Nevertheless, the court was told that the next defendant, Christopher May, was "an extremist, a member of the Birkenhead Communist Party, and a leader of the Birkenhead Young Communist League." The Prosecution added that he was extremely active in the work of the movement and had taken part in all the demonstrations. Two days before the incident in Bryanston Road, he had been arrested at another Communist demonstration and had been released on bail. May denied the allegations, saying that he was simply interested in protesting against the things which had jeopardised his living, such as the Means Test.

Richard Murphy, another of the defendants, denied the allegations against him. The court was told that he was not a member of the Communist Party, but that he had been in trouble before.

Summing up at the end of the trial, the judge said that the riot was a "tumultuous disturbance of the peace", and that there was every reason to accept the evidence of Inspector Williams. "The very worst friends of the unemployed are those who stirred up disorders," he added.

The judge went on, "It is suggested by the defence that the six police officers by themselves, without any pressure or attack upon them, suddenly went completely mad and drew their batons and attacked 2,000 people. Does the jury believe that that is true? The police faced a riotous mob and were outnumbered one hundred to one . . . "

His summing up lasted for an hour and a quarter, after which the jury left the court to consider their verdict. They returned 20 minutes later and brought a verdict of guilty against all the accused with the exception of Tighe and McAllister, who were immediately dismissed.

Sentencing Briggs to six months' imprisonment, the judge said, "You are not a leader but you took part in a very dangerous performance."

Murphy and May, who, the judge said, were beginning to think they were important people, were sentenced to borstal for three years. He went on, "If it were not for your youth (May was aged 19 and Murphy 20) I should have had to send you for a long term of imprisonment. You, May, seem to have got upon yourself a certain leadership among young people, leading them into a way which is as bad a way to lead decent unemployed men as can possibly be imagined. People who raise riots and demonstrations of this sort are the worst enemies of decent working men, and about 99 out of every 100 are decent."

As Murphy was dragged below he yelled, "Thank you Lord, thank you! Wait till I get out!" A woman at the side of the court screamed, "My Lord give him a chance," while in the gallery another woman collapsed and was carried out by the police.

Anderson was sentenced to four months' imprisonment.

The judge said the four men now remaining in the dock (Williams, McBeth, Greenwood, and Rawlings) were "Four of the worst enemies of their kind." He continued, "I don't know whether you wish to do good to working men, or whether it is that you are engaged in other activities not connected with work, but connected with revolution and terror, such as riots of this sort might induce among people liable to be stirred in that way. I regard you as dangerous people." Williams and McBeth were each sentenced to nine months' hard labour.

Addressing Greenwood, the judge solemnly said, "I wish to goodness I had not to sentence a youngster like you (he was aged 20). But you are misleading and drawing into riots, violence and bitterness, men who if they were left alone, would be decent men and decent workmen, and who really in their heart of hearts hate the cowardly sort of attack which was made upon the house of Baker . . . You will be kept in prison for 12 months' hard labour."

Joe Rawlings stood up of his own accord and moved to the centre of the dock after the last of his comrades had been taken below.

"You are," said the judge, "the secretary of the NUWM and an organiser of these grave disturbances. I know from my experience having sat in other Assize Courts on cases of this sort, of riots engineered, and deliberately engineered by the society of which you are the secretary, that they are the worst and most bitter enemies of decent workmen."

The judge sentenced Joe Rawlings to 20 months' hard labour. As he was dragged from the dock by the wardens, Rawlings shouted "My body goes to prison but my spirit lives in Birkenhead."

The sentences were extremely severe, particularly that on Briggs, who had received six months' imprisonment for merely taking part in the demonstration. Leo McGree appeared before the court some weeks later and received a similar sentence to that of Rawlings.

Rawlings himself was very bitter about his treatment at the hands of the courts. Years later he said, "It was a handpicked jury — middle-class and timid. A tremendous picture was painted about us, what fiends we were. Of course, he gave us stiff sentences — 20 months for me. I'd already been in remand for some weeks, so I reckon it was about two years altogether."

Rawlings had been held at Walton Prison in Liverpool before the trial, but served his sentence at Strangeways in Manchester and then at Wakefield. At the time, Wakefield held at least 26 Communist Party members, imprisoned for various offences ranging from riot to assault. This led to visits from Harry Pollitt, the general secretary of the Communist Party, and from Arthur Horner, the Communist South Wales miner.

Joe's 20 months' imprisonment was a grim experience, confined to a cell by himself. He spent his days in the ropery making string, and in the evenings he read one of the three books he was allowed each week. The only other respite from the daily grind of prison life was the monthly letter he received from home, and the monthly visit from his family.

CHAPTER NINE

Questions in the House

"They never would hear, But turn the deaf ear, As a matter they had no concern in."
Jonathan Swift

The most immediate consequence of the Birkenhead riots was that they sparked off similar disturbances across the Mersey in Liverpool[1]. On Wednesday 21st September 1932, fighting broke out in the Irish working-class district of Islington, near Scotland Road, as 3,000 unemployed followed Birkenhead's example. At a meeting organised by the Liverpool branch of the NUWM, a resolution was passed pledging to, ". . . fight against local economies and against the National Government, and to conduct a similar struggle in Liverpool. Further, to rally all Merseyside workers for the sending of a large local contingent to the National Hunger March to London for the opening of Parliament. We feel sure the success of the Birkenhead workers will act as the clarion call for the abolition of the Means Test and the defeat of the National Government of hunger and war."

The following day, further disorder occurred in Liverpool with another 14 people arrested in addition to the six already arrested on the Wednesday. Weeks later in Belfast and Glasgow similar riots broke out as the unemployed demanded an end to the Means Test and increases in unemployment benefit.

Events in Birkenhead and Liverpool soon came to the attention of Parliament when business recommenced after the summer recess on 18th October[2]. David Logan, the Labour member for Liverpool Scotland, asked the Home Secretary whether "his notice had been called to the recent civil disturbances in Birkenhead and Liverpool arising out of the unemployed demonstrations?" and whether ". . . he would be instituting an inquiry with the view to avoiding further clashes between civilians and police?"

Sir John Gilmour, the Conservative Home Secretary in Ramsay

MacDonald's National Government, replied that he was aware of the disturbances but had been advised that there was "no occasion for an inquiry."

Logan responded immediately. To Labour cheers, he asked, "Am I to understand that these troubles have arisen in regard to transitional benefit and on account of the poverty of the people, and that nothing is to be done to avoid clashes with the police when these people are taking up a justifiable attitude in regard to public demonstrations?"

The Conservative member Nancy Astor quickly came to the defence of her Home Secretary. She said, "May I ask if it is wise for Ministers in former Governments, who refused to see the unemployed when they themselves were in power, to advise these men to go on agitating?"

The Labour member for Westhoughton, Rhys Davies, then asked if a report had been called for from the Chief Constable. Taking up this point, Sir John Gilmour replied, "The Honourable Gentleman is no doubt aware that the police in the boroughs are controlled by Watch Committees and any complaint must be made in the first instance to the Watch Committee."

Determined to get an answer, Mr Davies continued, "Will the Right Honourable Gentleman be good enough to tell the House whether it is in the power of the Home Office to call for a report from the Chief Constable in cases of serious disturbances?"

"As I have already said," replied Gilmour, "as at present advised there is no necessity for my taking action."

Another reference that day to the Birkenhead riots came from James Maxton, the well-known Labour MP for Glasgow Bridgeton. He asked if the Home Secretary knew whether ". . . the police in the various districts who had been batoning the unemployed have been doing it under the instructions of the Home Office?" But the Speaker ruled his question out of order as it was superceded by another. And before Maxton could be reached again, time had run out for questions to the Home Secretary. However, a full debate on the riots was promised for the next day.

On 19th October, George Lansbury, Labour's Leader, opened the debate before a full House[3]. "Political democracy," he began, "is in danger of being wiped out altogether. At Birkenhead after the riots a great concession was made to the men who had gone there to demonstrate and at Belfast the same thing had happened." Lansbury added that he himself had been involved in many demonstrations but he did not support violence. He demanded that further concessions be made to the unemployed, and concluded his speech by saying, ". . . when you say that it is the Communists and the National Unemployed Workers' Movement who are stirring them up, they could not be stirred up if it were not for the conditions they are having to meet." He sat down to tumultuous roars of approval from the Labour benches.

The Home Secretary, replying for the Government, spoke of the aims of the NUWM and how it was Communist inspired. Revealing a thorough briefing in Communist affairs, he quoted from the 12th Plenum of the Communist International. This, he informed the House, "directs the special attention of all sections of the Comintern to the tremendous and ever-growing political significance of the unemployed movement which is being directed more and more against the capitalist state."

"The struggle of the unemployed," he continued, "has up to the present time been prepared by the Communist vanguard and organised by it to a much lesser degree than the strike struggle of the proletariat. The Communist Party and the revolutionary trade union organisations have not succeeded in organising serious mass activity by the employed workers in defence of the interests of the unemployed." This, he pointed out, conclusively illustrated the intentions of the Communist Party to organise the unemployed politically. By associating the unemployed and, in particular, the riots in Birkenhead with Communist directed tactics, he sought to lay the blame for the trouble with alien political forces.

Gilmour continued by confirming that the most serious incidents had occurred at Birkenhead and Liverpool. He added, "It was said in the debate to which we have just listened that the police today are adopting different methods of dealing with obstruction and with large crowds and with those who do not obey orders. On the other hand, it is worthy of note that at Birkenhead the technique of street-fighting, which has been advocated by the Communist International, has been considerably developed."

"For instance," he went on, "the police found at Birkenhead that trip wires — barbed wire in one case — had been stretched across the road about a foot from the ground, lights had been extinguished and manhole covers removed. These examples which I quote are constantly referred to with approval in the Communist press."

David Logan, the member for Liverpool Scotland, then rose and spoke of the problems of finding work, particularly in Liverpool where cheap "coolie and black labour" had replaced the more expensive white labour. He added that Liverpool was overrun with sailors unable to find ships.

"I speak not for the Communists," he emphasised, "but for men, whether they be Communists or anything else — men who have the right to live and have the right to proper treatment in a Christian land."

He continued, "The system of transitional benefit and the Means Test is immoral . . . The Archbishop of Liverpool denounced Communism only a short time ago. We are creating Communists daily by mismanagement and misgovernment in the working of a system that ought to be dead as a dodo."

Sir Stafford Cripps, the popular Labour member for Bristol East, also spoke against the Home Secretary. "What are we to say to the unemployed of Bristol who point to Birkenhead?", he asked. "We, who are daily trying to persuade them that they will achieve nothing by rioting, that they can only achieve by constitutional action, are met by the argument: 'But what is Birkenhead?'"

"Is anyone going to convince an unemployed worker," he continued, "who is told by a Communist that the only way he can force relief out of the local authority is by mass action, that these concessions have not been given as a result of force."

Ramsay MacDonald, formerly the Labour Prime Minister and now leading the National Government, closed the debate by saying that he recognised the problem but at the moment he was unable to do anything. He would, however, be making a statement on the Means Test in a week's time. Meanwhile, he appealed to all MPs not to encourage similar demonstrations as had occurred in Birkenhead.

CHAPTER TEN

Questions Elsewhere

"A man in a red shirt can neither hide nor retreat."
Hugh MacDiarmid

Back in Birkenhead, the allegations over police brutality
continued. At the Council meeting on 5th October, Alderman
William Egan complained about the behaviour of the police, but
his charges were quickly ruled out of order by the Chairman of
the Watch Committee, Conservative Councillor James Merritt,
who pointed out that they should not discuss the matter in detail
until the court proceedings were concluded.[1]

At the November meeting of the Watch Committee[2], a petition
was placed before members complaining about the conduct of the
police and asking the Council to hold an inquiry. This was signed
by the ratepayers of Flamark Street, Vine Street, Back St.Anne
Street, and Payson Street.

Alderman Egan, a Labour Councillor and former MP for
Birkenhead West, had been well briefed and delivered a long
series of allegations against the police to the Committee. He
began with the case of a man who had come home from work in
Liverpool and gone to bed at about 10.30pm.

"The door of his house was burst open by the police. He was
taken from his bed, batoned, and thrown into the police van clad
only in his shirt and trousers. He was remanded for eight days,
sent to the Sessions, and acquitted. He later lost his job and has
had no compensation."

"There was another case," he continued, "of a father and two
sons who had retired to bed. The father and one son were already
in bed and the other was undressing when the door was burst
open by the police and all three were batoned and taken away to
the Bridewell. They were remanded in custody for eight days,
and then one son was acquitted at the court, while the father and
son were acquitted at the Sessions."

"There was another man who was in bed at midnight. His door

was burst open and he was taken from his bed, and batoned so unmercifully that on arrival at the Bridewell the police surgeon ordered his immediate removal to hospital, where he remained for three weeks. This man has been ill for a long period with gastric trouble, and was actually on sick leave at the time. It was said that he suffered his injuries through jumping from one landing to another. But in point of fact that was a structural impossibility. Pictures and articles in the house were smashed, and the man's wife was batoned when she remonstrated. The daughter was threatened with similar action if she did not keep quiet."

"Another man named Sherlock, hearing a knock at the door, got out of bed and went down to answer it. As soon as he opened the door he was batoned and thrown into the police van. Before the van moved off, a detective looked inside and, seeing the man in question, said, 'You have got the wrong man'. He was returned to the house, but found that during his absence the table had been overturned and crockery and ornaments broken." That man had been given £5 compensation.

"A man named Warnock and his wife were in bed when the police burst open the door, overturned a table smashing crockery and ornaments and then tried to get up the stairs. The wife pushed a small chest of drawers on to the stairs to prevent the police's progress."

The list seemed endless, as Alderman Egan drew breath and continued. "Another man returning home was met by half-a-dozen policemen in Beckwith Street when he was not more than 20 yards from his house. He was knocked down and kicked while on the ground, and had to go to the doctor for attention."

"In another case three young men were standing in Watson Street on the Sunday evening, engaged in harmless conversation. The police van drew up, they were thrown into it, and taken to the police station and, after being remanded for eight days, brought before the court and acquitted. There was no compensation for them." Egan cited three more cases of innocent individuals being beaten up by the police, only to be acquitted by the court after spending eight days in remand. In a final case, Egan told of an eleven-year-old boy being attacked by the police in Storeton Road. As a result of being hit by a police baton, he had received a broken collar-bone. In all these instances no compensation had been offered.

In just four streets, said Egan, a total of 417 windows had been smashed. He alleged that "at one o'clock in the morning on Sunday 18th September, the police had visited Vine Street and broken 123 windows before proceeding to Flamark Street where 144 windows were smashed."

The Chairman of the Watch Committee was not impressed. Instead, he praised the police for their swift reaction to the disturbances, especially when they were so outnumbered by the rioters. At the end of the day a vote was taken and the call for an inquiry defeated by 32 votes to 20.

At a Council meeting on 7th December[3] awards were made to a police inspector and seven constables for "their courageous action on the attack at Baker's house". These were opposed by Labour, but carried by the Conservative majority on the Council.

The Chief Constable, Captain Dawson, made little mention of the disturbances in his annual report. He merely noted that, "In September, disorder of the gravest character broke out. This followed a long period of agitation by the so-called leaders who, it was evident, were influenced and urged on by outside sources, and would not be satisfied by other than aggressive methods. The disorder was promptly and efficiently suppressed, but, as invariably happens at such times, many innocent persons were involved in injury to property and person and the town is much mulcted in heavy riot damages. It is not a subject one desires to write about and I trust the occurrences may be forgotten"[4].

In the press the arguments raged. There were letters, statements, and counter-statements. But the attitude of the Establishment was best summed up by an editorial in *The Liverpolitan*, a local political monthly which was scathing over the concessions the Birkenhead Council had made and its climbdown in the face of force.[5]

"The Birkenhead authorities owe a duty to the town and to the whole country to stand firm and to postpone action as regards the relief scale and relief works until order has been restored by a superior force. To purchase peace by concession is to encourage the spread of disorder, as Liverpool soon found to its cost.

Communist propaganda must be stamped out as a deadly enemy of society. Its mission is wholly destructive and mischievous — and its method is to influence a few fanatical natures to act as leaders to permanently criminal elements. The Birkenhead outbursts were mainly criminal in purpose. The principal object in view was not justice to the unemployed, but loot. It is reassuring to find the trade unionists of Birkenhead repudiating the policy of violence. Let them go one step further — abandon mass deputations and leave their case to be argued by their duly-elected representatives.

The outbursts have lessons beyond those of the Criminal Courts. One of them is this: that it is unwise to permit a foreign-inspired, unconstitutional agitation to proceed day after day unchecked when thousands of men have nothing to do but to idle in the streets and market places. If the law is not strong enough to suppress Communist propaganda at a time like this, then the law ought to be strengthened forthwith.

A second lesson is this: it is bad policy to yield an inch to mob threats or to give ringleaders too much rope. Firmness at the first sign of illegal aggression generally saves trouble later. Deputations several thousands strong ought never to be argued with by public bodies. When a Town Hall is besieged it is time to call in the police, not to pass stupid, placatory resolutions. At such a stage discussion should be adjourned until law and order have been vindicated. Arguments should be listened to, but not when reinforced by threats and physical demonstrations."

Not only did this summarize perfectly the view taken by the National Government and its servants, but it highlighted an attitude towards concessions in the face of violence which still holds true today in similar circles.

Nor was there much sympathy from some sections of the Labour Party. Alderman Luke Hogan, the Leader of the Labour Party on the Liverpool Council, made his views quite plain.[6]

"We are not influenced in any way by our natural disgust at the attitude of a few extreme Communists who devote their time to reviling Labour's representatives instead of assisting us to secure control of the machine which keeps the people in poverty and subjection. We are with the unemployed body and soul and will strain every nerve to assist our people in every possible way. Disregard all those mischief makers who idly preach about communism and physical violence. Remember police batons have no soul and must be controlled by democratic influences."

But that was not the last to be heard of the disturbances. At a court hearing for Sidney Elias, Chairman of the NUWM and a leading member of the Communist Party, a letter was produced which was alleged to have been written by Elias in September 1932 when he was in Moscow organising the international unemployed movement. The letter was headed "Moscow".

"Now to take up one or two questions that I have been charged to speak about. Birkenhead. From the papers there is no clear indication that the movement is trying to break through the police terror. There is a great deal of talk about the spirit of Birkenhead and the fact is being overlooked that the police are successfully breaking Birkenhead's spirit.

Some proposals must be made to our comrades in Birkenhead and Liverpool on the methods of fighting the police terror. First the agitation must be continued in the streets . . . The NUWM branches there must organise on a street group basis. Get out leaflets, organise meetings where possible to keep the agitation growing.

Side by side with this we must work in the trade union branches and develop agitation for the dismissal of the Chief Constable, and in addition now and later — the Independent Labour Party (ILP) should organise a public inquiry at which these statements can be given publicly.

Trade union branches, co-operatives, Labour Parties and the ILP should be asked to send representatives to the inquiry. This work should be undertaken now in view of the fact that many of the lads are being sent for trial.

The National Administrative Council should issue a national call, in which we call upon the rest of the country to come into the struggle alongside the others, and very important that we raise the issue of employed workers, take strike action in favour of abolishing the Means Test.

Such strike action could be a one hour, one day strike. For example, we could concentrate on the anthracite area, the British builders, or the Liverpool dockers to secure such action. We should particularly work to get trade union branches drawn into the demonstration . . . "

Perhaps the Elias memorandum, like the Zinoviev letter of 1924, was a forgery conjured up by British intelligence to discredit the Communist Party and the Labour Movement. But there is no evidence to show this. However, if the Elias memorandum is genuine, it proves little. Elias was no doubt keen to exaggerate the role of the British Communist Party in the unemployed agitation to his foreign comrades. After all, in Britain the Communist Party had a membership of little more than four or five thousand, and in the 1931 general election it mustered only 74,824 votes[7], making it tiny in comparison to the Italian, French, German, and Spanish Communist Parties. And revolutionary activity in Britain was but a murmur compared to the earthquakes erupting on the Continent. So Elias would have something to gain by exaggerating the Communist Party's role in the riots of Birkenhead and elsewhere. The least it could do was to demonstrate a co-ordinated strategy of agitation across the nation. In February 1932, Elias had written in the *Daily Worker* that, ". . . by mass struggle in the streets, and by tremendous pressure on the Public Assistance Committees, we must compel the authorities to abandon the question of the Means Test."[8]

What the Elias memorandum highlighted, however, was the serious nature of the riots, and the importance placed upon them both nationally and internationally. The debates in Parliament, and the attention from Moscow, brought into the international spotlight the tragedy of unemployment in distressed areas such as Birkenhead. Repeated talk of hardship, and the extreme reaction which it had provoked on the streets, perhaps caused some politicians to reconsider their policies; it certainly caused countless members of the public, hitherto untouched by unemployment, to appreciate the depths to which many unemployed men and women had sunk.

CHAPTER ELEVEN
Conclusion: How Did it Happen?

*"They dreamed of riches in the rebel scheme
And find too truly that they did but dream."*
John Clare

How co-ordinated had the rioting in Birkenhead been, and was it inspired by the Communist Party? There is no simple answer to either question. Certainly, the NUWM was at the centre of all the activities among the unemployed. The Labour Party, divided by the defections of Ramsay MacDonald, Philip Snowdon, Jimmy Thomas, and others was unable to spearhead any effective Parliamentary campaign. The NUWM, by concentrating on the sole issue of unemployment, was able to draw in a variety of political activists.

Although at a national level the Labour Party was disorganised, at a local level in the towns and cities it was more actively involved in the protest against unemployment. And inevitably this protest brought them into close contact with the NUWM. Consequently, many ordinary Labour Party members and trade unionists worked in the NUWM. It would be wrong, therefore, to assume that the close relationship between the NUWM leadership and the Communist Party automatically gave it a Communist stamp. Yet there is no doubt that the Communist Party placed great importance on the NUWM and their participation in it. The majority of those controlling the NUWM and formulating its policies were members of the Communist Party. Indeed, the Communist Party was proud of its association with the NUWM; had the NUWM been controlled by any other organisation, there is no doubt that the Communist Party would have been far more critical of it, and of its leadership and policies. In the absence of such criticism lies the evidence of their close association. Nor was there any attempt by Wal Hannington to hide his connections with the Communist Party. On the contrary, time and again in his numerous books and pamphlets, he extolled not just the role of the NUWM, but also that of the Communist Party.

Yet this proves little. As far as Birkenhead is concerned, the local Communist Party hardly had more than 100 members, though they were, on the whole, active. Amongst them were people like Joe Rawlings and Leo McGree, both highly intelligent, capable men with a fair degree of organising skill. For a brief period in 1932, Rawlings was also a member of the National Administrative Council of the NUWM. But it would be wrong to place too great an emphasis on the role of these two alone, for, despite their skills in leading the unemployed, they could hardly have foreseen events or entered into any conspiracy to overturn the Means Test. They may have campaigned for such changes but, as pragmatic activists, they probably never imagined that they could achieve this end.

If anything, the disturbances in Birkenhead were unplanned and spontaneous. Certainly, there was Rawlings, the Communist Party, and the NUWM to give it a push in the right direction. But once the fury of the unemployed had been unleashed, there was little they could do to control events. In such situations force tends to adopt a momentum of its own and, in the event, Rawlings and his comrades had been taken out of the action before the conflict reached its maximum by their arrest. Undoubtedly, like any capable politician, Rawlings made the best of his circumstances, and his fiery rhetoric must have made more than a few hearts beat faster. But calculated or co-ordinated? No.

In the end, it was the unemployed and their families, frustrated by idleness, who reacted strongest. Certainly there were those who used the situation to their own advantage, and those who reckoned a punch-up with the police was a bit of fun. Criminals as well were inevitably drawn into the fracas and may even have initiated the looting. The widespread nature of the looting, however, suggests that it was simply a case of hungry people helping themselves to a free meal or a piece of much-needed furniture.

As for the police, they played their part in provoking the anger of the unemployed by their insensitive and uncompromising tactics. Birkenhead, with its history of disturbances, was no playschool for the police, and their behaviour certainly contributed to the violence. The numerous well-documented affidavits, rather than the less dependable oral testimonies passed down over the years, are sufficient to suggest that their reaction was largely unprovoked. However, the pressure on the Chief Constable from the Establishment was to be more forceful still in dealing with the situation.

It is the politicians who must take the greatest blame. It was their responsibility to be in contact with those who elected them and to be sensitive to their problems. Both at a national and a local level, those in power failed to heed the warnings and encouraged the slump by their ill-considered policies. That the politicians governing Birkenhead were able to overturn so quickly their previous policies on the Means Test and unemployment benefit indicates a lack of foresight and genuine concern for the unemployed. Once violence had flared, they all too easily reversed their positions. That it should have taken a riot to force them to acknowledge and react to the widespread desperation was indeed a neglect of their responsibilities.

The politicians in Birkenhead at least could argue, and with some justification, that they were merely carrying out the wishes of an elected Parliament. Ramsay MacDonald's National Government, on the other hand, had few excuses as it stumbled blindly through the Depression, implementing policies which merely aggravated the crisis, and then failing to react to the warnings. Indeed, it was not until the late 1930s that the threat of war and the policy of rearmament, with its massive public spending, boosted the prospects of employment.

On his release from prison, Joe Rawlings returned to Birkenhead.[1] With a prison record, his chances of finding work were slimmer than ever. He continued his work among the unemployed, and with the outbreak of the Civil War in Spain in 1936 he found himself a new crusade. Within a short time he had enlisted with the International Brigade, and along with 25 other Merseysiders was soon on his way to Spain. But he could hardly have arrived at a worse moment, and within days he was thrown into the front line at the battle of Jarama, one of the bloodiest and most crucial of the war. It was a grim experience and many, like Rawlings, who had arrived straight from the dole queues were physically ill-equipped for the rigours of such a battle. Months later, Rawlings and many others returned to England where they were able to campaign not only for Republican Spain, but also to warn of the growing threat of fascism.

When the Second World War broke out, Rawlings found work with Manganese Marine Limited, the propeller manufacturers in Birkenhead, and remained with them until his retirement. He continued as an active member of his union, the Foundryworkers, becoming secretary of the Birkenhead branch as well as secretary of the District Committee. He paid three further visits to the Soviet Union, and one of his final trade union duties was as delegate to the annual TUC conference. He stood many times as a Communist Party candidate in municipal elections in Birkenhead, but always received a very small vote. In 1978, after several years of illness, he died following a heart attack. His obituaries were brief; only among the unemployed was he remembered.

Whether the events in Birkenhead during the autumn of 1932 had much influence on the Government of the day is anyone's guess. MacDonald showed few signs of being affected by them, and was able successfully to lay the blame for the rioting at the door of the Communist Party and its militants. MacDonald's biographer describes the Government's attitude towards the unemployed as "pettifogging inhumanity".[2] By 1934, the Tories in MacDonald's Cabinet had foisted upon him a new and tougher Unemployment Act which was to cause such fierce protests throughout the land that the Government was forced to issue a standstill order. It seems that the lesson, if learned at all, was learned very slowly. The Means Test, which had embittered so many families in Birkenhead and elsewhere, remained a tool of Government policy until the 1941 Determination of Needs Act. Thankfully it has reappeared only as a shadow of its former self.

Afterword

The rioting which shell-shocked Liverpool and other parts of Britain during the summer of 1981, returned to our cities with a vengeance four years later. Streets and buildings burned in North London and in the Midlands; injuries were numerous; and a police officer was stabbed to death. The rioting in Liverpool might not have been as fierce in 1985, but it demonstrated the continuing ill-feeling between the city's police force and the community.

Just as resentment had burst into violence in Birkenhead in 1932, so it did again on Merseyside, with the police, once more, locked in battle. The anger of Liverpool's black community was born out of their frustration with continuing unemployment, poor housing, and social deprivation. This was much the same as the people of Birkenhead had experienced 50 years earlier. Their anger and aggression was not directed at the politicians of central and local Government, but focused on the police as the most immediate manifestation of authority.

This long chronicle of conflicts between Merseyside communities and the police is far from closed. With the Conservative Government now elected for a third term in office and with the gravest regional divisions, particularly between the North and South, the next decade may be an uneasy period for relations between the police and public. All the indications are that, on Merseyside at least, such confrontations have become a part of the culture, and look like remaining so for many years to come. Anger and resentment have passed down from one generation to another, with the name of the police tarnished for ever. Memories have lingered, and are rekindled every time tension and frustration rise in the community. Only by easing the tension will the anger subside. To confront it head on in the streets, as happened in 1932 and again in 1981 and 1985, will not solve the problem or reduce the bitterness. It will only add to it. These are the lessons which must be learned, from Birkenhead as much as from Toxteth, Handsworth, or Broadwater Farm.

References

Chapter One: Unemployment — The Crisis Looms

1. Galbraith, J.K., *The Wall Street Crash 1929* (Pelican, 1961).
2. *Ministry of Labour Report* Cmd 4281, Chapter 1 (HMSO 1932). See also appendix.
3. *Ministry of Labour Gazettes* for the mentioned years (HMSO).
4. Orwell, George, *Down and Out in Paris and London* (Penguin, 1963).
5. *Royal Commission on Unemployment Insurance* Cmd 4185 (HMSO, 1932).
6. *Ministry of Labour Report* Cmd 4281, Appendix V (HMSO, 1932).
7. *Ibid:* Chapter 1 "Extract on employment in various industries . . . shipbuilding and shiprepairing".
8. *Ministry of Labour Gazette* (HMSO, Sept 1932).
9. For further information on unemployment and its economic and social impact, see Branson, N. & Heinemann, M., *Britain in the Nineteen-Thirties* (Weidenfeld and Nicholson, 1971).

Chapter Two: Life Among the Unemployed

1. For a history of Birkenhead see the following: McIntyre, W.R.S., *Birkenhead, Yesterday and Today* (1948); Sulley, P., *History of Ancient and Modern Birkenhead* (1907).
2. Stewart-Brown, R., *Birkenhead Priory and the Mersey Ferry* (1925); McInnis, Jean, *Birkenhead Priory* (1983).
3. Between 1881 and 1921 the population increased from 84,006 to 147,800.
4. See Thompson, S.P., *Maintaining the Queen's Peace* (1958).
5. Report of the Chief Constable for the year ending December 31 1931.
6. Cammell Laird, Company Report 1931.
7. Cammell Laird, Company Report 1932.
8. Cammell Laird, Company Report 1933.
9. *Birkenhead News*, November 21st 1932.
10. *Daily Despatch*, September 24th 1931.
11. Quoted in Shallice, A., *Remember Birkenhead*, published by Merseyside Socialist Research Group. This is one of the few published articles relating to the Birkenhead riots of 1932.
12. *Birkenhead News*, September 21st 1932.
13. *Ibid.*
14. Birkenhead Public Assistance Committee Meeting Minutes, September 19th 1932.

15. Interviews — Belle Kelly & Mona Kelly.
16. Annual Report of the Medical Officer of Health for Birkenhead 1931.
17. Report of the Chief Constable for the year ending December 31st 1932.
18. *Ibid*.
19. Interview — Joe Rawlings.
20. Interview — William McCloud.
21. *Rothman's Football Year Book* (1983).
22. *Birkenhead News*, September 17th 1932.
23. Interview — Mrs Allison.
24. Interview — Mr McCloud.
25. Interview — Thomas Kelly.
26. Interview — Belle Kelly & Mona Kelly.
27. Shallice, A., *op.cit.*

Chapter Three: The Politics of the Dole Queue

1. Population Census of 1931 put the figure for 1931 at 147,946.
2. For a history of the NUWM see the following: Hannington, Wal, *Ten Lean Years* (Left Book Club, 1940); Hannington, Wal, *A Short History of the Unemployed* (Left Book Club, 1938); Hannington, Wal, *Unemployed Struggles* (Lawrence & Wishart, 1936); Hutt, Allen, *The Post-War History of the British Working Class* (Left Book Club, 1937).
3. For a history of the Communist Party see the following: Klugman, James, *History of the Communist Party of Great Britain*, Vols.1 & 2 (Lawrence & Wishart, 1968); MacFarlane, L.J., *The British Communist Party* (MacGibbon & Kee, 1966).
4. *The Labour Who's Who 1927* (Labour Publishing Company). To date no full biography of Hannington has been published.
5. MacFarlane, L.J., *op.cit.*
6. Ministry of Labour Gazettes.
7. Interview, Joe Rawlings. For further biographical information on Rawlings, see *Dictionary of Labour Biography*, Vol.8. *Rawlings, J.* by Stephen Kelly (Macmillan).
8. *Ibid*.
9. *Ibid*.
10. *Ibid*.
11. *Ibid*.
12. The *Daily Worker* later changed its name to The *Morning Star*.
13. For a more detailed biography of Leo McGree see Arnison; Jim *'Leo McGree'* (Union of Construction, Allied Trades & Technicians, 1980).

14. Interview, Joe Rawlings.
15. *Unemployed Special*, October 1932.
16. *Sunday Worker*, March 10 1929.
17. *Unemployed Special*, October 1932.
18. See also Hannington, Wal *The Problem of the Distressed Areas* (Left Book Club, 1937).

Chapter Four: Trouble Brews

1. Much of the information in this and the following chapters has been taken from local newspaper reports. These include the two weekly editions of the *Birkenhead News & Advertiser* and the daily editions of the *Liverpool Post* and the *Liverpool Echo*. Information also comes from interviews conducted with some of those involved in the rioting as well as minutes of the Birkenhead Council and the Public Assistance Committee.
2. McInnis, J., *'Birkenhead Park'* (Countywise, 1984).
3. *Birkenhead News*, August 6th 1932.

Chapter Five: "We Want Work"

1. *Birkenhead News*, September 10 1932.
2. *Birkenhead News*, August 20 1932.
3. *Birkenhead News*, September 14 1932
   and *Liverpool Echo*, September 13 1932.

Chapter Six: "Birkenhead's Communistic Reign of Terror"

1. Much of the information in this chapter is taken from the following:
   Birkenhead News, September 17 1932.
   Liverpool Post and *Liverpool Echo*, September 15 and 16 1932.
   Birkenhead News, September 21, 1932.
   Liverpool Post and *Liverpool Echo*, September 19 and 20, 1932.
2. *Birkenhead News*, September 17 1932.
3. *Birkenhead News*, September 17 1932.
4. *Birkenhead News*, September 17 1932.
5. *Birkenhead News*, September 17 1932.
6. *Birkenhead News*, September 17 1932.
7. *Birkenhead News*, September 21 1932.
8. *The Times*, September 19 1932.
9. *Liverpool Post*, September 19 1932.
10. Hutt, Allen *"The Post-War History of the British Working Class"* (Left Book Club, 1937).
11. Hannington, W. *"Unemployed Struggles"* (Lawrence & Wishart, 1936).

12. *Liverpool Post*, September 19 1932.

Chapter Seven: An Unexpected Victory

1. Much of the information in this chapter comes from the
   following;
   Birkenhead News, September 21 1932.
   Liverpool Post, September 19 1932.
   Liverpool Echo, September 19 1932.
   Liverpool Post, September 20 1932.
   Liverpool Echo, September 20 1932.

Chapter Eight: The Trial

1. Most of the information in this chapter is taken from the
   Birkenhead News, October 26 1932 and the *Birkenhead News*,
   October 29 1932.

Chapter Nine: Questions in the House

1. *Liverpool Echo*, September 21, 22 and 23.
2. *Hansard Parliamentary Debates, House of Commons*, October 18
   1932.
3. *Hansard, op.cit* October 19 1932.

Chapter Ten: Questions Elsewhere

1. *Birkenhead News*, October 7, 1932.
2. Minutes Birkenhead Watch Committee, October 1932.
3. Minutes Birkenhead Council Meeting, December 1932.
4. Report of the Chief Constable, *op.cit*.
5. *Liverpolitan*, October 1932.
6. *The Liverpool Post and Mercury*, October 1 1932.
7. Butler, D & Sloman, A. *'British Political Facts 1900-1979'*
   (MacMillan, 1980).
8. Quoted in Shallice, A. *op.cit*.

Chapter Eleven: Conclusion: How Did it Happen?

1. Interview Joe Rawlings. See also *Dictionary of Labour
   Biography*, Vol.7. *op.cit*.
2. Marquand, D. *'Ramsay MacDonald'* (Cape, 1977).